Justified by Her Children

Frank,

God bless you always

[illegible] +

October 2022

Justified by Her Children

Deeds of Courage Confronting A Tradition of Racism

Roy G. Pollina

Buena Vista, VA

1 3 5 7 9 10 8 6 4 2

Library of Congress Control Number: 2021903417

Justified by Her Children
By Roy G. Pollina
p. cm.

1. Religion—Christian Living: Social Issues
2. Social Science—Race & Ethnic Relations
3. History—United States: State & Local – South

I. Pollina, Roy 1951– II. Title.
ISBN 13: 978-1-7349136-3-7 (softcover : alk. paper)

Design by Karen Bowen

Whaler Books
An imprint of
Mariner Media, Inc.
131 West 21st Street
Buena Vista, VA 24416
Tel: 540-264-0021
www.marinermedia.com

Printed in the United States of America
This book is printed on acid-free paper meeting the
requirements of the American Standard for
Permanence of Paper for Printed Library Materials.

Dedicated to all the
Nuns, Deacons, Priests & Bishops
who guided me
to and through my vocation

Contents

"Yet Wisdom is justified by her children."

–Matthew 11:19

Acknowledgments

This book was made possible through the contributions and encouragements of a number of people, many from the loving congregation of Christ Episcopal Church in Martinsville, Virginia. The youth group of Phil Gresham's era are now the movers and shakers of today. My good friend, attorney John Swezey, was the person I turned to when I needed to know not just what happened but what it meant to the tightly knit community of Christ Church. I can never thank him enough for the insight he afforded me. And much the same can be said for the archivist of Christ Church, Sue Rosser. Not only was she able to recall her days as leader in Gresham's youth group, but she was able to provide the photos and paperwork for much of what she remembered. I am also deeply in debt to Charlie Cole, Ann Gardner, Trippi Penn, and Lucy Davis, who exercised their memories to recall the events of over six decades ago. My sincere gratitude goes to my friend Naomi Hodge-Muse for reading this manuscript and for introducing me to Michael Muse, who graciously provided insight into the difficulty of being a pioneer in the struggle for racial integration.

The research that went into *Justified by Her Children* could not have happened without the cooperation of Bishop Mark Bourlakas of the Diocese of Southwestern Virginia, who permitted access to the diocesan archives and his staff. The Rev. Canon Jonathan Harris and the Rev. Canon Mark Furlow set down their own work to open and close the vault for each of my visits. Just as I was beginning my research at the diocesan offices, the Rev. Nina Vest Salmon was winding down on her research on her doctoral dissertation. She was generous in sharing what she had learned that dovetailed with my writings. The research desk of the Roanoke Public Library was invaluable in helping me mine old news articles for informational gems on a host of topics. At the very end of the research process, I became aware of an article written by Phil Gresham in *The Living Church*. Through the efforts of Managing Editor John Schuessler, I was able to get a copy of this rare article from 1958.

There is not enough time to thank the publisher at Whaler Books, Andy Wolfe, for his confidence that this was a story for our time, if only I would work with an editor who could help me frame the story and keep it in that frame. Happily, Andy knew just the person, Lisa Tracy. Lisa's editing skills are remarkable. She knew where I wanted to take the story as if she had been down that path before I got there. It was a remarkable collaboration.

Two people require special recognition and thanks. I met with Bishop Light at his home when I was still on the edge of whether there was a story to be told or whether I was the right person to tell it. After our morning meeting, I drove to the diocesan office to drop off some paperwork for my church. I had just arrived when I was told that Bishop Light wished to speak with me on the phone. "You need to write this book," the bishop said. "That is all I called to say. You need to write it." At that moment, it was like the voice of God for me.

The final person I need to thank, and thank over and over again, is my wife, Susan. She gave me the time and space for the long hours of writing when I am sure there were other things I needed to do. She was my first proofreader and, I am happy to say, she remains my biggest fan. The feeling is mutual.

Foreword

Roy Pollina has written a sympathetic and incisive history of a particular period and place in Virginia. In 1954, following the definitive ruling by the United States Supreme Court in *Brown v. The Board of Education*, Christ Episcopal Church Martinsville and the Diocese of Southwestern Virginia began to face the deep pain of its own racism.

Slightly afterward, but almost simultaneously, major economic and industrial changes struck the region. Huge affluence was replaced by the rapid removal of the tobacco, furniture, and textile industries in a single generation.

The picture painted by the Rev. Mr. Pollina is of racism confronted and beginning to be overcome, of alienation between generations moving toward reconciliation, and the death of one culture pointing toward the birth of another.

–The Right Reverend A. Heath Light
IV Bishop of the Episcopal Dioceseof Southwestern Virginia

Introduction

Like a mutating virus, racism's destructive nature changes and morphs over time. Racism is at the center of *Justified by her Children,* a racism that existed almost three quarters of a century ago, but which still infuses and informs much that is happening across our nation today. Further, the racism of *Justified by Her Children* is a particularly ugly incarnation that may not be familiar to many readers who believe that churches were immune to this moral ill. With all of this in mind, our story will ask the reader to acclimate to "how it was" culturally in Southwestern Virginia in the mid- to late-1950s.

At the mid-point of the twentieth century, the city of Martinsville and its Episcopal Church were reaching a pinnacle of prosperity. The city's movers and shakers were, to a man, members of Christ Episcopal Church, and they were deeply religious, well-educated professionals, middle and upper class, and some, at the top echelons of Virginia political power—for the *Sturm und Drang* of racial strife within the purview of our story involved the best and brightest of Virginia. The people of Christ Church were law-abiding and church-going members of their society. It was their lot to live at a time when the law was dominated by Jim Crow and churches were expected to unquestioningly uphold an American culture in service of the white upper and middle classes. And as we shall see, the leadership of Christ Church embraced their white privilege with a tight grip.

It is important to understand "how it was," not to mitigate or excuse the destructive racism of the Jim Crow era, but to see that evil can be so dreadfully mundane that getting along with it seems the best way to get everyone to move forward. One thinks of Hannah Arendt's famous dictum that evil can be "terrifyingly normal," that otherwise apparently unremarkable people can be the agents of great harm. Into the mundane normality of Martinsville's Episcopal parish in 1956 came the Rev. Philip M. Gresham, and his experience in his new parish is used as the vehicle to tell the story of *Justified.* The youthful priest in his first call as a rector could have remained his parish's spiritual leader for many years as long as he provided the adults with edifying programs and the youth with sound instruction. It seemed a perfect match for the pastorally oriented Gresham, who loved liturgy, intellectual stimulation, and interaction with teenagers. He tried mightily to love and pastor the lay leaders who were resolute in upholding the inequality and separation of the races while professing a deep Christian faith and a steadfast love for their church. The sad end of this relationship—involving, of all unlikely things, a proposed summer camp for young people—came suddenly in a dispute over race in 1960.

Like all of us, the people who inhabit the history of Christ Church Martinsville are complex human beings. Sitting in judgment is always hazardous because sometimes heroes can have feet of clay, and even broken clocks are right twice a day. Readers will meet strident segregationists who gave their time, talents, and resources to the betterment of their church and community, although their myopic view of society limited their efforts to the white race. Moreover, there are proponents for racial justice who are sometimes reluctant to engage in the struggle, seeking instead compromises or work-arounds on the road to racial equality. In the end, the gift of the bishop's crozier, in itself both physically beautiful and slightly flawed is a fitting emblem of the redemption gained by a church that is both triumphant and scarred.

Gresham's young people are the lasting heroes of this story. In a long look back at a time few will remember, they can still teach us today about the justifying wisdom of getting involved. For them, too young to know anything else, "how it was" was "how it always was"—at least, how it always had been. But they were bright enough to wonder if it was how it was supposed to be. The Rev. Phil Gresham provided a vision of a future different from the racial division of their parents' community. Gresham gave them new ideas that diverged from their parents' thinking and a voice in their church to proclaim what they knew to be right. Gresham loved and respected the youth of his parish, and they returned his love and respect to the degree that half a century later, Phil Gresham is remembered by them as the greatest priest they ever knew.

May it give us hope.

–The Reverend Roy G. Pollina, 2020

1

Choir Practice Ambush

In 1956, in Southside Virginia's Martinsville, Charlie Cole had the dubious distinction of being the only boy in Christ Church's youth choir, an honor the high school sophomore and junior varsity football player could live without and had been trying to decline for several months now.[1] Charlie's father was a prominent member of the church as well as Charlie's Sunday school teacher, and Charlie knew it was expected that the Cole men would have leadership roles in whatever organization they joined. For the young Cole, this meant that at Christ Episcopal Church he would serve at the altar as an acolyte and sing in the youth choir.

While Charlie enjoyed serving as an acolyte with other boys his own age, he needed to get out of the otherwise all-girl choir. To this end, Charlie pointed out to both the choir director and his father that his voice had changed; he was no longer able to sing the high-register hymns selected for a majority girl choir. Charlie thought his argument convincing, but the adults in charge would have none of it. Charlie was ready to quit and quit now. Unfortunately for the reluctant choirboy, now was the worst possible time for the choir director, what with a new rector just arrived in town. The choir director was confident that he would make a better impression on his new boss with a mixed junior choir than he could with an all-girl choir, even if the mix was only one boy.

Football practice ran late this autumn night and Charlie was running late for choir practice. To add to his tardiness, the choir director had decided the young singers needed a full dress rehearsal rather than practicing in their school clothes. This evening, the junior choir members were to vest in their choir robes: a red cassock that reached to their ankles overlaid with a white cotta that reached to the waist. Full dress for the girls included a red beanie; in the Episcopal tradition women and girls were required to cover their heads in church. The choir room in the basement of the church was empty when Charlie arrived but he could hear the organ music and the soprano voices of the girls singing upstairs in the church. Charlie grabbed his cassock, the largest junior choir robe available, the one he'd worn last year that was supposed to reach to the tops of his shoes. It didn't. Looking down at the red hem more than a few inches shy of his ankles, Charlie thought here was another

Junior Choir 1954–1955

reason to leave the choir; he had outgrown even its largest vestment. He buttoned the top half of the thirty-three buttons on the cassock, one for each year of Christ's life, and pulled the white cotta over his head as he made his way to the basement door. In order to get to the nave of the church, he had to exit the church basement, going outdoors to climb several short flights of stairs between the rectory and the church. The athletic high school sophomore took the stairs two at a time and reached the street at one of the two main entrances to the sanctuary.

He stopped at the sidewalk and bent over to fasten the last few buttons at the bottom of his cassock. "Nice dress, Charlie, or should I say, Charlene?" came a jeering voice from behind him. Charlie looked up to see three boys in Martinsville varsity football letterman jackets standing in front of him on the Church Street sidewalk. It was impossible to know which one made the remark prompted by his choir outfit, nor did it matter, since all three were chuckling at the cheap shot.

"Get lost," Charlie shot back while trying to make his way to the church's front door.

"What's that, Charlene?" needled one of the three as they continued to have their fun at Charlie's expense.

Charlie Cole would one day become a star defensive player at VMI who famously sacked Navy's star quarterback, Roger Stauback; he was not the type to back down from a challenge, except, perhaps, when he was standing at the door of his church. He pushed his way past one of his antagonists and was promptly and roughly shoved back by one of the others. The pushing match between the two only lasted a moment before turning into a melee of three against one. It did not take long before Charlie found himself on the front lawn of the rectory warding off blows and throwing a few well-placed punches of his own. Choir vestments were not designed for street brawling and proved as much a hindrance to Charlie as being outnumbered.

The fight was not going his way. The flash of light he saw from the side door of the rectory was more likely from a glancing blow to his left eye, though he thought he saw a shadowy figure in black moving toward the scrum of boys rolling on the grass. Suddenly, one of Charlie's attackers went flying away. In less than a second, another of his assailants disappeared from on top of him. Charlie was able to throw off the last boy by himself. He scrambled to his feet to see his three attackers lying on the ground in front of a short, blond-haired man dressed in black.

"You boys go on and get to your homes," said the man as he handed one of Charlie's attackers his MAVAHI baseball cap. The three lettermen helped each other up and started off without a word down Church Street.

Quickly brushing the dirt and grass off his crumpled cassock, Charlie mumbled an unsure "Thank you, Mister Gresham," to his priest. To his relief the young rector's face lit up with an understanding smile.

"You're welcome. And, please, it's Father Gresham, OK?"

"Thank you, Father Gresham," Charlie replied over his shoulder as he turned and hurried into the church for what was definitely going to be his final choir practice.

I had been in Martinsville only a couple of months when I met Charlie. We both had been invited by the residents of Scuffle Hill to the Brunswick stew boil that took place every autumn behind the church, and that was the evening Charlie told me the first of many stories I would hear about the Rev. Philip M. Gresham. His account of the ambush made it easy to understand why this priest was so memorable. Over the succeeding months I would hear many more Gresham tales. Often, these stories about Gresham either began or ended with the attestation, "the greatest priest I ever knew." Most of the storytellers were septuagenarians, recalling the young priest who had made a deep impression on them in their high school years. They would admit that their high opinions of Gresham did not always coincide with those held by their parents, especially the fathers of the boys. The adult males in Gresham's church, it seemed, had their suspicions about the priest's sexual orientation—this at a time when anything other than heterosexual relations was illegal, considered sinful, and something never to be brought up in polite conversation.

While the men of the congregation held their tongue about their doubts regarding Gresham's sexuality, they were less reserved about where he might lead the congregation when it came to race relations during this period of legal segregation. In the mid-1950s, as events unfolded, it would become clear that the powerful men of the church's vestry led by a state Supreme Court justice as senior warden, were not going to allow their congregation to become part of what they saw as a clergy-driven social experiment of "a mingling of the races"—this at a time when the majority white population had put laws in place that made eating at the same lunch counter a crime.

Many of the heroes of the civil rights movement were African-American men who had earned the title "Reverend." Often, the planning of marches and demonstrations against segregation was organized in their church basements. The historic black churches won acclaim for leading the fight for racial equality and became targets for the racial hatred of the segregationists. Mostly untold and thus largely forgotten is that in the white churches, segregationists and integrationists fought each other in an unholy battle over the soul of the institutional church. The sad historical record of white religious denominations is that many of them looked upon their black members as an inconvenient problem, best to ignore until sometime in the future.

In this racially charged atmosphere, the Rev. Philip M. Gresham would strive to fulfill his duty as a cure of souls, to bring peace and unity to his conflicted congregation while remaining loyal to his priestly vow to proclaim the Gospel of equality and dignity for all of God's children. Gresham's time as rector in Martinsville, especially his work among its youth, provides the framework for a story that challenges our understanding of "how it was then"—a phrase I would become quite familiar with in my tenure at Christ Church—but also of how it is now. The challenges that the young priest faced remind us that racism can exist in the person who kneels in the pew or holds the chalice or teaches Sunday school.

Now as then, there are those who will argue that there are "some very fine people on both sides" of the racial divide without probing what that means.[2] It was during the 1950s that psychologist Leon Festinger gave the world the term and understanding of cognitive dissonance. Professor Kathleen D. Vohs, describing Festinger's work, states that cognitive dissonance "occurs when conflict emerges between what people want to believe and the reality that threatens those beliefs. The human mind does not like such inconsistencies: They set off alarms that spur the mind to alter some beliefs to make the perceived reality fit with one's preferred views."[3] Half a century has not diminished the cognitive dissonance we endure in our attempt to try to make sense of race relations, church and culture, sexual orientation, the flaws of our leaders, and the hope that we place in our youth.

It was shortly before I retired, as I prepared for the baptismal instruction of a young couple with a new baby, that I recalled one of my first such instructions as a parish rector. It was a disturbing memory not happily brought to mind; a time when I was called upon to deal with the power of that cognitive dissonance between what we believe and what we choose to remember.

As the rector of a parish in southeast Louisiana, I eagerly set forth that day to prepare the family for their baby's baptism.

They were the type of family every church wants to cultivate: young married homeowners with a new baby, working hard to build a good life. They had a modest house on an impressive piece of property outside of town. He supervised the groundskeeping at a local country club, and she was occupied full time with the care of their first child. We sat in the living room and spoke quietly, my visitation purposely planned around the baby's nap time.

I said a short prayer to begin and handed them each a copy of the Book of Common Prayer. We opened it up to the baptismal vows and, one by one, we read each vow and I translated the formal ecclesiastical phrasing into common English. We easily worked our way through the Apostle's Creed, a familiar understanding of Christian doctrine. I explained that the vow about continuing in "the apostles' teaching and fellowship, in the breaking of the bread, and in the prayers" meant that they would remain faithful members of a church, go to Communion on Sunday, and pray daily. Each vow received a brief explanation with an opportunity for questions and answers.

Everything went as expected; I had been well trained in seminary. Confident in our progress, I put the last two vows together with my textbook explanation of what the Christian understanding of those vows entailed: Will you seek and serve Christ in all persons, loving your neighbor as yourself? Will you strive for justice and peace among all people, and respect the dignity of every human being?

"You see," I said, "the Christian understanding of baptism is that every Christian pledges to love, serve, and respect others. One could hardly be a member of the Ku Klux Klan and be a good Christian."

This explanation and example were my best efforts to make plain an important Christian principle that I fully expected to pass without question or comment. "Well, I don't know about that," the young man started. "My Uncle Billy was a Grand Cyclops in the KKK, and I think an excellent Christian. He was a favorite with all of the cousins because he would take us hunting and fishing. He was a deacon at his church, there every Sunday. I know he read his Bible." He paused in fond remembrance. Then: "I think Uncle Billy was a good Christian."

Although I had lived in the South for over a dozen years, this Chicago transplant was totally astounded that anyone, especially a reasonably well-educated young Christian man, would defend a member of the KKK, even if it was Uncle Billy. Not prepared for this discussion, I somewhat cravenly switched illustrations. "All right," I said reaching into a more familiar example from where I grew up, "let's agree that you cannot be a good Christian and a member of the Mafia."

"Agreed," came the response without hesitation, and we moved on. After a few housekeeping items about protocols like no flash photography in the church and arriving early on the day of the service, we finished our instruction on baptism just as the baby awoke.

I live with the guilt that I should have done better for that family than just changing the metaphor to something we could all agree on. Being a "good Christian" was something that this young father admired in his Klansman uncle without ever recognizing the impossibility of that position. I often wondered how the church, how I, could have overcome his way of thinking about Uncle Billy—a way that was rooted in family relationship, happy memories, and contradictory membership in a hate organization. Would recognition of the dissonance that Uncle Billy represented ever emerge for that father or, especially, for his child, who was almost certain to grow up influenced by his father's point of view? Growing up with his father's family stories, the great-nephew of Uncle Billy might well never doubt that being a member of the KKK and being a good Christian were possible. Nearly two decades after his baptism, he might not have any doubt that there were "some very fine people on both sides" at the August 2017 encounters between white supremacists and people opposed to Confederate statues in Charlottesville, Virginia. How could it be any different? Any attempt to throw shade on the memory of Uncle Billy or Uncle Billy's crew could only be the result of "fake news." For his great-nephew, "how it was" with Uncle Billy is an absence of family memory of fiery crosses, obscured by the blurred lens of stories about fishing trips with the cousins. I pray that, if I were called back to a church in Chicago, I would not give in to the need to revise my baptismal instruction again and switch my example from the Mafia back to the KKK because of someone's memories of likable Uncle Tony "the Enforcer."

As George Orwell told us in his dystopian *1984,* "Who controls the past controls the future; who controls the present controls the past."

2

Virginia is for Lovers

I was blessed to be the rector of Christ Episcopal Church Martinsville, Virginia, from September 15, 2011, until June 30, 2015. After 26 years of ordained service in the Diocese of Louisiana, I had decided to accept the call to Martinsville. I had been through one hurricane too many in Louisiana, that one hurricane being named Katrina. My wife, Susan, and I immediately fell in love with the Virginia countryside. After spending thirty years in southeast Louisiana, a place where they have five different words for flat, I never cease to be amazed at the majesty of the misty, forest-covered Appalachian mountains. My soul delighted in the tranquility of the nearby Blue Ridge Parkway. My spirit feasted on the timelessness of the Shenandoah Valley. The state's welcoming sign proudly proclaims, "Virginia is for Lovers." For Susan and me, Southwest Virginia was love at first sight. We immediately sought to learn everything we could about our adopted state.

Among the best-known facts about the history of the state of Virginia is that the state was home to many of the nation's founding fathers. First and foremost is George Washington—commanding general of the Colonial Army that defeated the British in the War for Independence, first President of the United

States, and "Father of His Country." Second only to Washington is Thomas Jefferson, author of the Declaration of Independence and the nation's third President. There is little that can dim the honored memory of these bright Virginian stars of American independence. Little, but not nothing. For like other prosperous Virginians, these founding fathers of the land of the free were, paradoxically, slave owners. In Virginia, wealth was in the hands of the plantation owners with their vast fields of tobacco and other cash crops. The prosperity of these agrarian enterprises required cheap labor to till the soil, plant the seed, and harvest the crop. On the Southern plantation, slavery was the required engine for producing riches, a system of forced labor of mainly black Africans oppressed by white landowners. The wealth and the scale of these enterprises built upon bondage could sometimes grow to enormous proportions. George Hairston, who fought with General George Washington at Yorktown, was one of the richest landowners in Virginia, owning 238,000 acres in Henry County alone[4]—where Martinsville happens to be the county seat. By 1851, a Richmond, Virginia, newspaper claimed that a Hairston was the richest man in Virginia and maybe the entire United States. It is estimated that prior to the Civil War, the entire Hairston clan, by then spread from Virginia throughout the South, owned multiple plantations worked by an estimated 10,000 slaves.[5]

In 1858, the Republican candidate for the US Senate from Illinois used Scripture to make his point that "a house divided against itself cannot stand." Candidate Abraham Lincoln added, "I believe this government cannot endure, permanently half slave and half free." He lost that election. His honest assessment in his "House Divided" speech was a truth few were willing to hear.

Five bloody years of the Civil War ended in freedom from slavery for African-Americans, but not freedom from inequality.

The defeat of the Confederacy meant the end of slavery but not of the social and the cultural prejudices used to justify that "peculiar institution." The Bureau of Refugees, Freedmen and Abandoned Lands, known as the Freedmen's Bureau, struggled to help the newly freed slaves adjust to life off the plantation. Created by Congress in 1865, the Bureau was unable to overcome the white privilege that continued to oppress former slaves in the old Confederacy. Black workers found little relief in white courts for claims on unpaid wages or for physical abuse by white employers. Freedman schools for black children were subject to harassment; teachers were threatened. A Freedman's school in Martinsville was closed after a month; a school in Lexington was burned to the ground.[6] Overwhelmed by opposition, the Bureau ceased operation in 1872. In 1896, the United States Supreme Court ruled in *Plessy v. Ferguson* that racially separated facilities did not violate the US Constitution as long as those separate facilities were equal. Ultimately, "separate but equal" was a failure because it was a fraud.

As the new rector of Martinsville's Christ Church, much of what I was learning about Virginia was adding to a body of knowledge I had gained over a lifetime of interest in history. Still, it is one thing to know history, and another to feel a part of it. I was born and raised in Illinois, "the land of Lincoln." Even though half of my life had been spent in the South and my children were proud Southerners, it was hard to shake the reputation of being a Yankee transplant. I could not change where I came from, but I tried mightily to root myself in where I was now. Along with the macro-narrative of Virginia I wanted to learn the micro-history of the parish that I was called to pastor.

When I made my move to Martinsville I had a remarkably short resume. Of the 26 years of ordained ministry, 23 had been spent in a single parish outside of New Orleans. Two decades-plus is an unusually long tenure for an Episcopal priest in a single parish. As I was to find out, at Christ Church Martinsville, a long tenure was all but unheard of. In my first weeks there, I was waiting to begin the regular Wednesday noon Holy Eucharist service in the small chapel in the undercroft of the church. There I was greeted by John Swezey, a local attorney and a long-time devoted member. John was one of the people I would quickly get to know and like. John said he had something to show me and proceeded to walk me across the floor of the large meeting room that the church used for its dinners and congregational meetings. Displayed on the far wall were two parallel rows of dozens of framed pictures that ran the length of the room. Here were portraits and photos of all of the rectors of Christ Church dating back to the 1840s. Swezey walked me to the middle picture and pointed. “See this man?” he asked, then continued without waiting for a reply. “He was rector when my family arrived in Martinsville in the mid-1950s.” With a sweep of his arm, Swezey indicated the dozen pictures to our left: “These are all of the rectors before my family arrived, going back over 100 years. And these,” Swezey swept his arm to the right, taking in half of the pictures on the wall, “are all of the priests who have been rector since I arrived.”

A quick check of the names and dates on the small brass plaques under each picture told the tale. In over 170 years of its existence, half of the priests called as rector to Christ Episcopal Church had served in the last 60 years. The rectorship of a priest at Christ Church from the 1950s forward generally lasted four to five years. Two of the frames included men I recognized as priests who went on to become bishops, but most of the rest were priests who spent only a handful of years at Christ Church before taking their leave for greener pastures or being told by the vestry to move along. I asked Swezey if there was a particular favorite priest among those hanging on the wall. Swezey did not hesitate nor did he have to move from where he stood. Pointing to the likeness of the youngest priest on the wall, the photo next to the portrait of his first Christ Church rector, hung the photo of the Reverend Philip M. Gresham, 1956–1960. Swezey turned to me and spoke with great intensity, "That is the greatest priest I ever knew." Thus, I was introduced to the enduring admiration of the Rev. Gresham that was widely shared by a group of parishioners who had been teenagers in the late 1950s.

Philip Gresham's family had deep roots in Henry County, Virginia. His great-great-great grandfather Philip Anglin came to America from France about the year 1750, accompanied by his son, Philip Anglin II, a boy about 10 years old.[7] Philip Anglin II married, and for a short period lived in Henry County. In 1797, Philip Anglin III was born in neighboring Patrick County, where he grew up and farmed land about eight miles northeast of Martinsville until his death. John B. Anglin was the son of Philip Anglin III; it was John who moved to Martinsville and lived at 205 Starling Avenue.[8] John married twice. His second wife, Pocahontas Houchins, had six children with him, their youngest being a daughter they named Grace. John and Pocahontas lived in Martinsville until about 1920 when they moved to Holdenville, Oklahoma, to be near their oldest son, W. T. Anglin. Things had gone well for W. T. He was a prominent politician serving over a long career as a state senator, speaker pro tem of the Oklahoma Senate, lieutenant governor, and acting governor of that state. It was sometime around the Anglins' move to Oklahoma that William Dew Gresham, living in Martinsville and teaching at Henry County's first and oldest public school, Ruffner Institute, met and married Grace Anglin.[9] Eventually, Gresham moved his family to Richmond for a teaching position; there in 1927, Philip Morton Gresham was born.

To complete the historic circle, in less than 30 years, Philip Gresham would return to Martinsville as the rector of Christ Episcopal Church.

3

"People Would Not Understand 'How It Was'"

There are two types of people when there is mention of Martinsville: Those who repeat, "Martinsville?" and those who say, "Oh yeah, Martinsville." The former are probably 99 percent of the US population; the latter are NASCAR fans who know that Martinsville is the home of "the paperclip racetrack," smallest track on the NASCAR circuit. It was less than five miles from the track that one of my life's most significant occasions would take place. And unlike Phil Gresham, I was one of the 99 percent. I had never heard of the city of Martinsville until I saw Christ Church's "position open" posting for a new rector.

Now I was about to take my place as rector of Christ Church, a position first occupied in 1841 by the Rev. George Washington Dame. To bestow this honor upon me, the Right Rev. F. Neff Powell, fifth bishop of the Diocese of Southwestern Virginia, had driven the 60 miles to Martinsville from the diocesan office in Roanoke. For my part, I had relocated 850 miles from Covington, Louisiana, to accept this call. Although I was a seasoned priest with 25 years of ordained ministry, I could not escape the excitement of a new church, with new people under the authority of a new bishop. I was still in the early days of learning about my new home. Bishop Powell would bring a whole new dimension to my education at my installation that night.

The church was filled for the grand occasion of installing a new rector. The congregation of Christ Church, from the loyal to the curious, turned out in large numbers. The small congregation of, the traditionally African-American St. Paul's Episcopal Church, Christ Church's sister church in town, was well represented and warmly received. The stately procession into the church included the distinguished local clergy vested in their liturgical finery as well as a representative contingent of Episcopal priests and deacons from the diocese. Bishop Powell closely followed the order of service as prescribed by the Book of Common Prayer and copied in the freshly printed pew sheets. Episcopalians are known for doing everything "decently and in order," as the Apostle Paul recommended. So it came as a surprise when the bishop interrupted the normal flow of the service and called the children forward for a brief, unscheduled children's sermon. The children gathered around their bishop and sat against the altar rail to hear a story. The story he told this night was one of the bishop's favorites and oft repeated: the story of the Bishop's Crozier.

As the children settled in, Bishop Neff Powell held out his crozier for all to see. The stylized long black shaft with a silver crook was an ancient symbol of the bishop's authority. Powell told the children how for many years the bishops of the Diocese of Southwestern Virginia did not have a crozier, until the youth group at one of the churches decided to raise money to buy the bishop a gift. Those were troubled times in the diocese, when the bishop was deeply involved in the struggle for civil rights and the end of racial discrimination. Many parishioners in the diocese did not want their bishop to be so involved, and they were very angry at him. But the young people at this one church decided they needed to show their bishop that they believed he was doing the right thing for everybody. So as a gift, some would say as a peace offering, the youth group purchased the black and silver crozier and presented it to the bishop at a diocesan youth gathering. The year was 1960—here Bishop Powell paused for effect—and the church youth group was from Christ Episcopal Church in Martinsville.

That night at my installation was the first time I heard that amazing story, but it was not the last. Bishop Powell delighted in telling it, and I would hear it a few more times before he retired and returned to his home state of Oregon. When the diocese elected its sixth bishop in succession, the Right Rev. Mark Bourlakas added a second, more modern, more reserved wooden crozier, less ornate and more like the wooden shepherd's crook that a crozier was meant to be. Though the the silver crozier was still in use, the story of the brave young people of the Martinsville youth group who gave it started to fade, a piece of oral history no longer repeated. Surely, I thought, this story must be written down somewhere; churches love stories like this and write them down all the time.

Crozier in case

Over the months, the story of the crozier replayed in the back of my mind like a favorite hymn. As the rector of Christ Church, I decided that it was my duty, possibly a divinely inspired invitation, to write a few pages to keep this memory alive. I could not let the tale of the bishop's crozier just fade away; it was too good to be forgotten. I confided to a few members that I was contemplating writing a brief history of the gift of the crozier for the church's archives. But instead of the delighted encouragement I expected to receive, I was told that I might want to reconsider and write about something else. The story of the crozier with its brave teenagers standing with their bishop for a good cause, I would learn, was a bit darker than in Neff Powell's children's sermon. I was warned time and again, "People would not understand 'How it was.'"

4

Revisiting How It Was

So how was it? It is probably safe to assume that most of the children sitting at Bishop Powell's feet understood the simple moral of the story of the crozier, which is that people, even teenagers, can seize the moment to be brave and do the right thing. The moral of the story, courage in the face of adversity, was quite clear. Understanding the history, the "How it was," was considerably more difficult. I was about to attempt to write a brief history on a subject I had only just learned about from a children's sermon. "How hard could this be?" I confidently thought. I could easily write a brief history of the crozier as I went about my regular work as a parish priest.

Bishop Powell's children's sermon properly focused on the presentation of the crozier as a peace offering without dragging the children into the narrative weeds of a long, complex, and sometimes bloody history. I quickly found that it was not possible to honor the gift of the crozier without at least attempting to revisit how it was for those young people and their favorite priest. To understand the full measure of the "peace offering" of the Christ Church youth group, one needs to understand the historical context surrounding Christ Episcopal Church in Martinsville, Virginia, that made the tale of the crozier special. The church, the city, and the state each have a story to tell.

Newcomers to Martinsville and the surrounding Henry County will be excused for not understanding the love and passionate devotion that longtime residents have for their community. A quick tour of the area passes deserted storefronts, half-empty strip malls, and abandoned factories. In 2016, the local newspaper, the *Martinsville Bulletin,* reluctantly admitted that things were pretty bad in its part of Virginia. The paper reported that "when an aspiring photojournalist wanted to take some meaningful black-and-white photos of a cracked, weedy parking lot, they would come to one of our shuttered furniture factories."[10] Martinsville was easily "a poster child for economic woe" and a "cautionary tale of the downside of NAFTA." Yet the longtime residents who remember the boom years during and after World War II speak with a fondness for their hometown that is as endearing as it is difficult to imagine, given the current situation.

The traces of the glory days of Martinsville can still be seen in the magnificent homes that grace the city's historic district and line Mulberry Road. Viewing these stately homes with their manicured lawns and circular driveways, it is easy to accept the locals' often-repeated boast that during the 1950s Martinsville had one of the highest concentrations of millionaires of any city of its size in the country. Back in the day, Martinsville was the area's dominant municipality. When Martinsville became involved in an industry, it owned that industry. Martinsville was a city that was not afraid to reinvent itself. When the economic environment changed, Martinsville evolved with it until it became the dominant species. From the "Chewing Tobacco capital" to the "Furniture Manufacturing capital" to the "Textile Manufacturing capital," the citizens of Martinsville prospered with each change.[11] In 1900, there were as many as 14 plug tobacco factories in Martinsville.[12] When chewing tobacco's popularity gave way to the cigarettes made in nearby Winston-Salem, North Carolina, the local tobacco workers learned new skills in the furniture manufacturing plants that were taking root in the area, such as Bassett, Hooker, American, and Stanley. About that same time, textile companies, eager to take advantage of a skilled workforce, began building manufacturing plants in the area. Pannill Knitting, Sale Knitting, and Bassett-Walker Knitting were among those bringing prosperity to the residents. But the unchallenged heavyweight of the textile industry in Martinsville was the DuPont nylon factory, employing as many as five thousand workers.[13] Opened in November of 1941, it attracted employees from all over the country, known to natives of Martinsville as the "DuPonters." In the late 1950s, the citizens of Martinsville took dubious pride in the widespread rumor that their town's largest-in-the-world nylon factory had a Soviet nuclear intercontinental ballistic missile aimed at it.[14]

John Swezey's family were "DuPonters"; they moved to Martinsville while John was still in grade school. Besides being a devoted churchman, Swezey was well known as a student of, and a predictable, spontaneous lecturer on, local history. He was my go-to person when I struggled to understand Virginian culture or had questions about the history of Martinsville and Christ Church. I knew I would need his help to write the story of the crozier, so I visited Swezey at his office to ask his assistance.

After some friendly banter, he became totally engaged when the topic of racism came up. Swezey's blue eyes flashed with intensity as if the force of his words would enable 21st century hearers to understand what the culture of racism was like in 1950s Martinsville. "There was a black side of town, we didn't think otherwise," he began. "Globman's was the big department store downtown and Leggett's department store, too, they had the water fountains, White, Colored; they had restrooms, White Women, Colored Women. It was just the way it was. You didn't think anything about it. You just thought that that was the way it was supposed to be."

A few hours after leaving Swezey's law offices, I visited the Fayette Area Historical Initiative, a museum of African-American history in Martinsville. One of the attendants, who looked to be the same age as Swezey, proudly showed me the exhibits on display in the small storefront museum. Displayed prominently on a wall was a picture of the first black Miss Virginia, a resident of Martinsville. My guide told me of the two Martinsville residents who were members of the heroic Tuskegee Airmen fighter squadron of World War II. I was told that the first bank on the black side of town was founded by a Buffalo soldier, a member of the African-American cavalry units formed after the Civil War to protect settlers heading west. Besides their own bank, the blacks of Martinsville had their own medical facility. I viewed pictures of the building that held St. Mary's Hospital on one floor, a pharmacy on another floor, and a "beer joint" on another. The museum had a presentation on the history of the Baltimore-based Jobber Pants Company, which brought well-paying industrial jobs to black agricultural workers coming to the city for work. All during the tour my guide never once tried to delineate or modify by race any of the organizations or enterprises on display. He did not speak of the black theater, or the black hospital, or the black school. He spoke of the theater or the hospital or the school "where everybody went."

As I was learning, when a white person referred to the something "everybody in town" did in the 1950s," he or she was using shorthand for "every white person." The same held true for an African-American who spoke about "everybody," but meaning "all black people."

There were few exceptions to this way of speaking, but one—and it was notable—was the Gymtorium.

When black rock-n-roll headliners like Chubby Checker were booked into the Gymtorium, everybody went to see them. This time, "everybody" actually meant everybody—only this time racial segregation was turned on its head. The main floor of the Gymtorium would be packed with black teenagers, while the white teenagers were permitted to rock out from the balcony—a reversal of how it was in many theaters and even many churches. Rock-n-roll gave young people of any race something to agree upon. But when the music stopped, in school, in church, in restaurants, everywhere in Virginia in the middle of the twentieth century, the races were once again separated, culturally and legally. Those who remember the history of the beginnings of rock in the 1950s may also recall in retrospect how many white people of the older generation were shocked and incensed by this music that was actually crossing over from the black culture of the South. As John Swezey was trying to help me understand, at least in the memory of many who lived it, all of this was "just the way it was" and you "didn't think otherwise."

It became increasingly obvious that in order to write about the crozier I had to understand how it was for Gresham's students. I constantly needed to remind myself that the racial milieu of the southern states of the old Confederacy was qualitatively different from that of the rest of the country. I needed to remind myself that I lacked the race consciousness that Southerners carry with them as part of their heritage. In telling the story of how it was for Gresham's youth, I needed also to attain a self-understanding of how it was for me. I needed to come to grips with the fact that, when it came to racism, I did not know what I did not know.

My awaking to racism did not occur until the summer before my senior year of high school. I grew up in a quiet suburb on the west side of Chicago that was affluent enough to provide modern, clean, and academically above-average public schools. Still, my parents chose to send my sisters and me to the Roman Catholic parochial school, no small feat on the single income of a barber. At St. Eulalia School, I received a superior liberal arts elementary education built on a solid moral and religious foundation. This also meant that my circle of social contacts was limited to white Roman Catholic children who lived in a white Chicago suburb. I was a sophomore in public high school before I ever sat at a desk next to a non-Christian, or a Protestant Christian for that matter. I was away at college before I could make a similar statement about any race other than white.

Prior to college, my first sustained encounter with African-Americans my age occurred the summer I was 17. Before our senior year in high school, my girlfriend decided to go to a regional Catholic youth event, and I decided to tag along. The region in this case was the archdiocese of Chicago, a religious province that covered some of the most racially segregated geography in the country. The plan was to bring together black high school students from the city with the white students from the suburbs in the hopes of breaking down racial barriers. It did not start out well. The event was standard church youth group camp. We would listen to a talk about a topic with religious, social or moral implications and then break into small groups to discuss the issues. The most important issue I had to deal with on the first day was to wind up in my girlfriend's small group. Successful in that endeavor, I found myself sitting on the floor in a hallway with her, two white girls from the suburbs and three African-American girls from Chicago. I waited for introductions to end before I announced that I would fetch some drinks for everyone from the cafeteria in the other building. Unfamiliar with the campus, I wandered a bit; still, I was gone for less than ten minutes. When I returned with our drinks I found all six girls sobbing heavily, black girls on one side and white girls on the other. I slid over to my girlfriend on the floor.

"What happened?" I asked breathlessly.

She turned, fighting back tears. "They said the ice cream cones were racist!" She struggled to control her voice. "How could ice cream cones be racist?"

One of the white girls agreed, "Nobody thinks about race when they eat an ice cream cone."

A black girl on the other side of the circle shook her head in protest, "You don't know how it is. This sort of thing happens all of the time. You just don't want to see it."

I remembered the carton of drinks and started to hand them out, "I have no idea what happened while I was gone. Would someone please explain it to me?"

The third white girl, silent to this point, explained. "We were talking about racism. I said that racism was disappearing after Martin Luther King and all the work he had done." The girl nodded toward one of the African-American girls. "She said that there was almost no letup on racism, and that it was everywhere she went, even when she bought ice cream. She said that everyone knows that when you ask for a cone with one scoop of vanilla and one scoop of chocolate ice cream. The white vanilla scoop is always placed on top of the brown chocolate scoop, and never the other way around, because white always has to be on top of brown."

The African-American girl who had made the statement about the ice cream spoke next. "That's right. Just like I said. That's how it always happens. Quiet racism, pure and simple!" The other black girls nodded their agreement.

At this a white girl objected. "That's not true, nobody thinks like that when getting ice cream. I know we don't."

"You may not," said a black girl, "but I bet you cannot find an ad or any picture of an ice cream cone with chocolate and vanilla scoops that is different than white on top, brown on the bottom."

By now all weeping had stopped, and some quiet, though intense, conversation was taking place—no doubt the type of conversation the program people had in mind in setting up a mixed raced conference in the summer of 1968. Before that day, I never heard that dispensing ice cream could be racist. I learned years later that some Southern towns would not permit black children to eat vanilla ice cream. I also learned that the song many ice cream trucks played as they rolled down the street, "Turkey in the Straw," was a favorite tune of minstrel shows, often sung with racist lyrics with revised titles like "Zip Coon."

As I researched the story of the crozier, I kept in front of me the memory of what I had learned that day about the perception of racism in the dispensing of ice cream. I tried always to be aware that having been a white, middle-class child of the Chicago suburbs had made me oblivious to most of the systemic racism around me. I did not know what I did not know. If Gresham's students had any advantage over me, it was that in Virginia, racism was an ever-present part of the culture of education. In Virginia, the schools were a major battleground over racial integration, beginning in the mid-1950s.

The census of 1950 showed that African-Americans were just a little over 20 percent of Virginia's population. The majority 80 percent, overwhelmingly white, constructed a legal caste system based on their belief in the inferiority of the black race.[15] The Commonwealth's attorney general, Lindsay Almond Jr., had won a case in federal court for Virginia's segregation laws, only to have that case appealed and grouped with another case coming out of Topeka, Kansas, in 1954. The United States Supreme Court, in its unanimous decision in *Brown v. the Board of Education of Topeka,* ruled that the laws establishing "separate but equal" classrooms in public schools were unconstitutional and ordered the racial integration of schools nationwide. The Supreme Court's decision in *Brown* was more than just a matter of law; the ruling challenged the order of Virginia society.

Aware of the cultural consequences of the high court's order, Virginia's elected representatives were not slow to push back with a series of legal maneuvers aimed at thwarting the impact of *Brown*. Virginia state Sen. Garland Gray headed a commission charged by Gov. Thomas Stanley with finding a way around the integration order. The commission devised a two-part solution. The first part was to allow local jurisdictions to manage desegregation locally, assigning pupils to schools as they saw fit. Second, in accordance with the commission's view that students should not be required to attend a mixed-race school, parents were given tuition grants should they decide to choose an alternative education for their children.[16] This "local option" plan allowed for some integration of the races, although the actuality of that happening was highly unlikely.

For Virginia's Democratic US Sen. Harry F. Byrd, the Gray Plan was deficient. He declared that *Brown* was itself an unconstitutional attack on states' rights, and on February 25, 1956, he called for what would become known as "Massive Resistance."[17] The Virginia General Assembly met in special session in 1956 to cobble together a package of legislation to put Massive Resistance into effect. These laws, named for Virginia's governor, were known as the Stanley Plan. The Virginia Historical Society goes on to tell us that, "A Pupil Placement Board was created with the power to assign specific students to particular schools. Tuition grants were to be provided to students who opposed integrated schools.

"The linchpin of Massive Resistance was a law that cut off state funds and closed any public school that attempted to integrate."[18] In a few counties in Virginia, the local boards of education took the drastic step of shuttering their schools rather than integrate them. In the counties where the schools were closed, most white children enrolled in newly instituted private schools, while most black students and the poorer white students stayed home with no school to attend. To get their children an education, black parents sent their children to other states to live and go to school. Other families were forced to lie about their residency on enrollment applications in Virginia counties that still ran segregated schools. In 1957, the Virginia attorney general who had argued before the Supreme Court for segregation in the *Brown* case, Lindsay Almond Jr., became governor with 63.2 percent of the vote. When federal judges ordered the integration of public schools in Fort Royal, Charlottesville, and Norfolk, Gov. Almond kept his campaign promise to support Massive Resistance and closed nine schools, locking out nearly 13,000 students.[19]

The mass closing of schools became a tipping point.[20] Many parents wanted to find another way to deal with the school crisis other than giving up on the public school system. Leading businessmen in the state told their governor that the crisis was adversely affecting Virginia's economy. When Governor Almond lost two lawsuits challenging the school closings, one federal and one state, in one day, January 19, 1959, he moved to repeal the closing laws and permit desegregation. For one Virginia county, it took until a 1964 Supreme Court ruling to reopen public schools there, and it took another Supreme Court case in 1968 before large-scale desegregation took place in Virginia.[21]

The segregation of the schools in Martinsville was pretty typical of the rest of Virginia. Outside the city of Martinsville in Henry County, in the basement of the Fayette Street Christian Church, a small high school for black children was established as early as 1900. In 1917, The Rev. Albert Harris arrived in Martinsville and eventually became the principal of a free school for black children, the Martinsville Training School, with grades one through seven. It was not until 1939 that a high school for African-Americans entered the public school system in the Martinsville area. By contrast, the all-white Martinsville High School on Cleveland Avenue was built thirty-five years earlier, in 1904. Then, in 1958, four years after the US Supreme Court ordered the desegregation of schools, Martinsville constructed a new building to house the all-black Albert Harris High School.[22] Finally, nine years after the Supreme Court ruled that racially separate but equal schools were unconstitutional, Martinsville High School enrolled its first black student, Michael Muse. Though not a member of Gresham's youth group, Muse was an Episcopalian, their classmate, and, as we shall see, a mover and shaker in his own right.

In the spring of 2018, I met Michael Muse for breakfast at one of Martinsville's coffee shops. The meeting was arranged by Michael's stepmother, who was also the local president of the NAACP, Naomi Hodge-Muse. In 2012, Naomi and I had been chaperones on a youth mission trip sponsored by Christ Episcopal Church to Katrina-ravaged, still recovering, New Orleans. Hodge-Muse suggested that if I wanted to know about school integration in Martinsville, I should talk to the one who knew it best from personal experience. For an hour on a Saturday morning, Michael Muse revealed what it was like to be the first black student—he early on told me that he preferred the word black—to integrate Martinsville High School.

When he enrolled in 1963, Michael Muse was the first and only black student in Martinsville High School. It remained that way for the entire year. At the time, the high school encompassed five grades, eighth through twelfth; Muse was an eighth grader when he integrated Martinsville High School. Escorted by the police into the school, Muse entered the building with the expectation that he would be protected throughout that tense first day. Taking his seat in the balcony for the opening day school assembly, Muse discovered the police escort gone, leaving him unprotected. Realizing that he might be at risk without his escort, Muse left the balcony for a safer location just as the program started. Later, Muse heard the rumor that the retreat of his escort was part of a plan to have him kidnapped that first day. Whether false rumor or thwarted abduction, Muse showed he was trained to protect himself. Once his parents decided to choose the all-white Martinsville High School for Michael's education, he was sent to Chase Western Reserve University in Cleveland, Ohio, the hometown of Michael's mother. For three months he studied at the University "to get him up to speed" academically for the transition to the white school. Equally important, Muse was enrolled in a special program that trained him in the techniques of nonviolent resistance. Muse appropriated most of what he was taught about nonviolence, but not everything. His reluctance to absorb completely a nonviolent stance was a disappointment to his father, a prominent leader in the local civil rights movement.

"I had my own code," Muse confessed. "My code was that I would never fight over anybody calling me a name," he said, "but if somebody spat or hit me, I would fight back. I didn't care what I was taught to do."

Muse paused to catch a clear memory: "I did not have that experience until two or three weeks later." He then related an episode at the beginning of a gym class where four boys attacked him. A fifth boy leapt to Muse's defense; Muse and his defender held their own until the teacher entered and stopped the attack. All six were sent to the principal's office and all six were given in-school suspensions for fighting. The white students who befriended Muse over the year were the target of racial slurs by some of the other students, but by graduation in 1968, Michael Muse had gained the respect and friendship of most of his classmates. He was vice president of the Debate Club, and the National Honor Society honored him for Outstanding Achievement Among Negro Students. Muse would go on to college in the fall, and that same year Martinsville would finally close its black only schools permanently.

One of the factors that worked in the community's favor for racial harmony during the integration of the schools was the construction of a new education building that had never been an all-white nor an all-black school. When it opened in the fall of 1968, the school administration was cautious to not stir up any racial competition. A good example of avoiding racial conflict was played out at the school's homecoming. The school had an integrated homecoming court but no homecoming queen, thus avoiding the situation of choosing between black and white contestants for the royal high school crown. Racial tension could not be totally avoided. In 1968 there were one black and three white students running for each of the four class offices in the junior class. None of the white students could be persuaded to drop from the race, so the white vote split and the black students won.

The student body took the election in stride, and white students shrugged it off with, "Well, we knew that would happen."[23] This sentiment was not shared by some parents and other white residents outside the high school community, who complained about the vote. Racial attitudes outside the boundaries of the school could be toxic for these teenagers. From time to time, the administration was called upon to protect its students from racial slurs when the integrated classes took field trips in the area.

Given the sometimes-violent history of school integration in other parts of the country, Martinsville did better than many in ending segregated public schools. Still, it should be noted that 1968 saw the opening of another Martinsville school along with the new high school. That fall saw the opening of Carlisle, a new private school with an all-white student body.

5

A New Priest for Christ Episcopal Church

As the textile and furniture manufacturing center of Southwestern Virginia, Martinsville in the 1950s was a hard-working industrial city—working every day, that is, except Sunday. On Sunday, Martinsville kept the Lord's Day and went to church. In their Sabbath-keeping, the citizens of Martinsville were little different from most of their fellow countrymen. This was a time when Americans believed that faithful church attendance was their civic duty, protection against a world where their religious way of life was being threatened by godless ideologies. When Nazi Germany was marching through Europe, President Franklin Roosevelt called on Congress and the American people, declaring that "four essential human freedoms" were under attack. "The second is freedom of every person to worship God in his own way—everywhere in the world," he emphasized.[24]

But the defeat of the Nazis and the end of World War II did not end the threat of godlessness; America found itself immediately drawn into a Cold War with atheistic Communism. Just before his inauguration, President-elect Dwight Eisenhower argued that the Communists would never understand America's democracy because they lacked the religious principles for that understanding. Few loyal citizens would disagree about the importance of religion in America even though Eisenhower was uncomfortably noncommittal about what form the American religious foundation took. "In other words, our form of government has no sense unless it is founded in a deeply felt religious faith," Eisenhower said, then mystifyingly concluded, "and I don't care what it is."[25]

For the spiritual seeker, choices were plentiful in Martinsville. All of the mainline Protestant denominations were represented as well as a Roman Catholic church and a Jewish synagogue. But the polestar in this religious constellation, as anyone who had lived in Martinsville for any length of time knew, was Christ Episcopal Church: the church to belong to, the denomination of community leaders, of movers and shakers.

In a state where history is almost a currency, any Episcopal parish had a distinct advantage in attracting the most prominent worshippers. Starting with Jamestown in 1607, the Commonwealth of Virginia's history included an established church, the Church of England. In colonial Virginia, conformity to the Church of England was required by law for all government officials and indeed all citizens, thus forcing Presbyterians, Methodist, Baptists, and others to become scofflaws. While it might be possible to skip Anglican worship to attend a church of choice with impunity, there was no safe way to avoid the taxman. The taxes collected by the British Colonial government went to build and repair Anglican churches and to pay the Anglican clergy.

In an early show of Colonial defiance, patriot Patrick Henry came to prominence in a lawsuit involving the clergy's tax-paid stipend. That allowance was tied directly to the price of tobacco, the colony's principal source of wealth. In a year of poor harvest, an Anglican parson's stipend rose at the very time when his congregation was suffering the most. When the colonial legislature, the House of Burgesses, sought to end this disparity and their legislation was vetoed by King George III, Henry took on the defense of the colony's right to make its own laws. The 1763 case of "The Parson's Cause" became in effect one of the opening engagements between the colonists and the king that would lead to the American Revolution.

Following the colonists' victory in that War for Independence, the Virginia Commonwealth's new legislature, the General Assembly, ratified Thomas Jefferson's historically famous Statute of Religious Freedom to ensure that no future government in the Commonwealth would try to dictate how its citizens worshipped nor support any religious practice with citizens' taxes. Disestablished and detached from the Church of England, the American Anglicans reorganized themselves as the Episcopal Church in America in 1789. The newly minted Episcopalians of the Diocese of Virginia quickly enthroned their first bishop, James Madison (cousin of the President with the same name), in 1790,[26] and many if not most prominent Virginians continued to kneel in what had formerly been Anglican churches and adhered to an American revision of the Anglican Book of Common Prayer—deleting prayers for the King's Majesty and offering prayer for the President and Congress.

With the dawn of the nineteenth century, the population of this new American enterprise pushed farther westward to found villages and towns away from the cities of the Atlantic coast. Over time, despite their new-found religious freedom, the citizenry of these new communities often seemed tacitly to agree that the former Anglican, now Episcopal, churches were still the province of the affluent and well-positioned—and anyone aspiring to join them. Founded in 1841, Christ Episcopal

Church in Martinsville shared its first rector, the Reverend George Washington Dame, with a congregation in Danville 30 miles to the east.[27] In 1848, the small Martinsville congregation built its first house of worship on West Church Street, on land donated by Marshall Hairston. Though in their own building, parishioners continued sharing a rector well into the mid-1850s, when the Reverend John R. Lee is recorded serving both Christ Church and Trinity Episcopal Church in Rocky Mount, 30 miles to the north. After a series of rectors, Christ Church was blessed in 1894 with the 26-year rectorship of the Reverend Alfred W. Anson. Anson was the son and grandson of Church of England priests, his grandfather dean of the cathedral in the ancient city of Chester and his father, the Reverend Frederick Anson, canon to Queen Victoria. Alfred's nephew, William Temple, would become the Primate of the Church of England and the Anglican Communion.[28] In May of 1903, The Rev. Anson and his congregation had a new hilltop church built on land donated by Miss Ann Marshall Hairston, daughter of the church's first land

Christ Episcopal Church, 1950s

donor. Neither the generosity nor the influence of the Old South's ruling families had diminished at the dawn of the 20th century.

Its location at the top of Scuffle Hill made it topographically the highest church in Martinsville, and this placement was not an accident. It was said that when the United Methodist Church bought property higher up the hill on Church Street, placing it seemingly closer to the heavenly places, the Episcopalians sold their property lower down the hill and below the Methodists to claim the top of the hill.

Much credit for the new church went to the chairman of the building committee, Judge Stafford G. Whittle—a family name important to this narrative that would recur at many key moments of the church's life in the years ahead. Indeed, when Philip Gresham arrived as Christ Church's new rector, he would find his vestry was a veritable "who's who" of Martinsville, and its senior warden would be Judge Kennon Whittle, son of Judge Stafford Whittle. Almost 200 years after the Revolutionary War and the disestablishment of religion in Virginia, the Episcopal Church of the 1950s was, arguably, still the "right" church to belong to in the Old Dominion.

Its preeminence was not without real merit, moving forward from the early to mid-twentieth century. The Reverend Charles Cochran Fishburne Jr., DD, began his long and successful ministry as rector of Christ Church in the spring of 1935.[29] At a vestry meeting in January of 1936, Fishburne chose Judge Kennon Whittle to help organize a men's Bible class that later became known as Christ Episcopal Church's Laymen's League. By the 1950s, the Laymen's League's Evangelistic Outreach program was a quintessential example of the power and prestige associated with Christ Church in Martinsville. The programs put on by the Laymen's League were not your average church's Bible study. An archival history of the League recorded, "The events lasted a week and featured such speakers as Dr. C. H.

Dodd of Cambridge University; Henry Luce, editor of *Life, Time,* and *Fortune* magazines; and Dr. Reinhold Niebuhr of Union Theological Seminary. Regarding these events, Dr. Niebuhr said, 'This is the greatest expression of religion I have ever seen.'"[30] In 1952, Dr. Arnold J. Toynbee presented three lectures on "A Historian's View of Religion." In 1953, the featured speaker was Dr. James Mullenberg from the faculty of Union Theological Seminary in New York. Christ Episcopal Church, its archives assert, "was in the eyes & ears of the country because National television covered the sessions, all the Virginia newspapers, *Time* & other magazines."[31]

The widely recognized success of such programs was among the achievements that led to the Rev. Fishburne being awarded the honorary degrees of Doctor of Humane Letters from Roanoke College and Doctor of Divinity degree from Washington and Lee University.[32] So it was no surprise to anyone when Fishburne received one of the highest honors a priest can attain, a nomination for bishop in his own diocese, the Diocese of Southwestern Virginia.

But it was not to be. While it is almost certain that Fred V. Woodson, a Christ Church vestryman and a member of the Special Electing Council of the Diocese, was influential in making Fishburne a candidate for bishop in the election of 1953, there was a crowded field of eight contenders and Fishburne was lost in the pack. After five ballots, the choice was announced: the new bishop of Southwestern Virginia would be the Rev. William H. Marmion of Delaware. Perhaps it was this loss—Fishburne had to be disappointed that he never received more than two votes from his brother clergy—or perhaps it was, after twenty years, just time for a change. Whatever the reason, Fishburne accepted a call from Tryon, North Carolina, in 1956, tendering his resignation at Christ Church and precipitating the call process for a new rector.

In the 21st century, an Episcopal congregation seeking a rector has access to the profiles of every Episcopal priest through a computerized data base at the national church headquarters in New York City. The "open parish" will spend weeks preparing their own profile under the guidance of a trained transition specialist sent by the bishop. The parish profile is matched to the clergy data base, generating a list of qualified priests. Before the rector is chosen there will be months of meetings for combing through questionnaires and intensive background checks, and reviewing phone and/or Skype interviews—all leading to personal visits with a very short list of candidates from which a rector is chosen. The process usually lasts a year or more. Even when this method of calling a rector produces a good result, often both the priests and the Call Committees learn to hate the process for being exhaustingly long and complicated.

In the middle of the 20th century the process of calling a priest was local, short, tightly controlled and often done with a nod and wink from the bishop toward a favored candidate. The calling process of the 1950s had all of the pitfalls and temptations of favoritism and prejudice associated with using a "good old boy" network. Still, when compared with present-day methodology, the church's former selection procedure was faster, and its results probably no better or worse, than the current high-tech process that takes five times as long.

As it happened, at a special meeting of the Christ Church vestry on June 3, 1956, their bishop's voice was heard in a report of the Call Committee on the search to replace the Rev. Dr. Fishburne.[33]

The minutes of this meeting state that the vestry reviewed an "unsolicited letter from Bishop Marmion in which the bishop suggested and endorsed the name of the Rev. Phillip Gresham, assistant to the rector of St. James, Richmond, Virginia, as a possible successor to the Rev. Dr. Fishburne." It would have been extremely bad manners not to honor the bishop's recommendation, so by unanimous vote of the vestry, the Rev. Gresham was invited "to conduct Holy Eucharist at Christ Church on Sunday, June 10, 1956." There was also discussion around another candidate for rector, the Rev. George Holmes, associate rector at St. John's Roanoke, Virginia, but no invitation was extended, leaving us to forever wonder about that discussion. Soon after the meeting, Justice Whittle sent a letter to Marmion about the action of the vestry in accepting his endorsement of Gresham for their next rector. On June 11, 1956, the bishop responded to the senior warden of Christ Church and admitted that he had not met the priest in question, his lack of intimate knowledge made somewhat evident when Marmion referred to him in the letter as "the Rev. Philip P. Gresham"; Gresham's middle name was Morton. Still, Marmion confided that "he has been highly recommended to me, and I trust you will find him admirably fitted to meet the needs of our church people in Martinsville." The bishop sent a copy of the letter to Christ Church's junior warden, Fred V. Woodson, whom Marmion knew from Woodson's service on the Bishop's Call Committee.[34]

But as the process moved forward, for a time at least, everything seemed to be working against Christ Church and Philip Gresham getting together. Justice Whittle had to inform the vestry that Gresham was on a two-month leave from St. James Church until "the latter part of July and, therefore, was unable to conduct Holy Communion at Christ Church on June 10, as planned."[35] The vestry was not to be deterred. Plans were made for Gresham to "conduct Holy Communion at Christ Church early in August, upon his return from England." Again, the vestry's plans were frustrated by the Episcopal clergy's common practice of taking vacation during the summer months.

When Gresham returned to St. James he was forced to decline the vestry's "invitation to conduct Holy Communion at Christ Church any Sunday during the month of August because the rector of St. James, Dr. Gibson, is away on vacation" and Gresham was "committed to conduct services at St. James."[36] Despite frustration over the scheduling conflicts, Christ Church continued their pursuit of St. James's curate because the background checks and references on the Rev. Gresham were encouraging. Justice Whittle reported in August that "excellent recommendations" to the Call Committee had been received on Gresham's behalf. Among these from his undergraduate days came a note from Earl Mattingly, the treasurer of Washington & Lee University, who highly recommended Gresham.[37]

Despite the vestry's apparent eagerness, it could be argued at this point that for such a young clergyman, the Rev. Gresham might have been advised to be grateful for all the help he could get; Christ Church had a prestigious pulpit, and he was not alone in being considered for the position. Christ Church Martinsville was a cardinal church, one of the handful of churches in a diocese that have the money, people, and influence to make or break any program proposed for the entire diocese. Not surprisingly the Christ Church Call Committee was receiving the names of priests who wanted, or whose supporters thought deserved, the power and influence, not to mention the challenge, of being a "cardinal" rector at Christ Church. Recommendations had come in for the Rev. Ralph Wood Smith Jr., rector of St. Anne's in Wrightsville Beach, North Carolina, and for the Rev. Douglas E. Wolfe, curate of Trinity Church Portsmouth, Virginia, and both were also being considered.

Whether it was cagey strategy on Gresham's part or just the circumstances of life, the delays started to work in his favor. Unable to get Gresham to come to Christ Church in Martinsville for an interview, the Call Committee appointed a delegation of three vestrymen—C. P. Kearfott, R. M. Simmons Jr., and Stafford G. Whittle III, to attend morning services at St. James in Richmond on Sunday, August 12.[38] Joining this delegation were parishioner John K. Adams and vestryman M. K. Jacobs and his family. The next day the group gave a full report to the vestry on the results of their trip. They began with a brief biographical sketch of Gresham: He had graduated from Washington & Lee University in 1949; served in the armed forces; graduated from Virginia Theological Seminary in 1952; and was a young bachelor. Finished with a mere outline of Gresham's life, the group all but bubbled over in their enthusiasm for the priest they had met in Richmond. They proclaimed that not only were they "favorably impressed by Mr. Gresham but also, being convinced that he is exactly the man for the vacancy at Christ Church," they recommended "that the vestry should extend a call to him immediately!" Theirs must have been quite a presentation because the vestry unanimously accepted the enthusiastic report and then unanimously voted to extend "immediately" a call to Gresham to become rector of Christ Church. In a highly unusual move the vestry then voted to offer to the 29-year-old priest, ordained less than five years and without prior experience as a rector, "the same salary and allowances" as had been paid and allowed to the proven, long-termed the Rev. Dr. Fishburne at the time he resigned, a compensation package that included a salary of $6,000 a year plus a rectory with all utilities, plus about $600 a year car allowance, standard pension, vacation, and other benefits.[39] There was no denying Christ Episcopal Church earnestly believed they had found their man, The Rev. Philip Morton Gresham.

6

Getting Ready for the New Rector

In the Episcopal Church, it is not unusual for both the clergy and the laity to use marriage as a metaphor for the relationship between the rector and the congregation. The canons for the Episcopal Church give the rector essentially a life tenure at his or her post. Those same canons require that the priest retire at age 72, but, unless there is a legal or moral violation, the rector's position with the congregation is for all intents "until we are parted by death" or until retirement age. For their part, the congregation calling a priest believes that their call can only be "a marriage made in heaven." What happens after the call is accepted is, not surprisingly, known as "the honeymoon period." During this early phase, usually lasting 12 to 24 months, the new rector can get the leadership of the congregation to consent to or to try just about anything. The leadership, for their part, is anxious to show the congregation what a good job they did in the calling process, so just about anything the new rector does is promoted as evidence of their brilliance. Inevitably, the honeymoon period ends, and two disappointed parties settle into a reasonably happy arrangement with their flawed partner. As one veteran priest put it, "During the first twelve months of the rectorship the priest and the vestry try to figure out who stretched the truth the most on their profiles."

Perhaps sadly, as with civil marriages, few clergy and congregations today stay together through to the end. The average tenure of a priest with a congregation in the Episcopal Church is roughly five years, approximating marriage in America. As more than one counselor has observed, much that we believe about marriage is a mirage. Yet, though the years of wedded bliss may prove to be an illusion, the beginning of the union is an occasion of joyous optimism, which is why congregations love this metaphor when they call a priest.

And in the 1950s, an era when divorce was still very much frowned upon in civil society, marriage was very much the operative metaphor for the church's call process. At Christ Church, the more congregants learned about the Rev. Philip Gresham, the more their anticipation rose.

There is some uncertainty about Gresham's early years. One biographical sketch says he was educated in the Richmond public school system.[40] The report to the Christ Church vestry states, probably incorrectly, that Gresham attend Virginia Military Institute before entering the Army.[41] Several contemporary accounts state that Gresham served in the armed services from 1944 to 1946, although the US archives show he enlisted on July 2, 1945.[42] Finding accurate information is always a little dicey since, by their own admission, over a third of the government's Access to Archival Database (AAD) records are incorrect. There is universal agreement that Philip Gresham attended Washington & Lee University as an undergraduate after the war, where he joined their wrestling team. He graduated from Washington & Lee in 1949.

What we know about Philip Gresham's religious upbringing comes from an unsigned account in the Christ Church archives of a first meeting with Gresham. One of Christ Church's Sunday school teachers writes, "He was not born into the Episcopal Church. He studied different religions and chose to be an Episcopalian and he really knew everything about the church."[43]

Gresham received his Bachelor of Divinity degree from the Virginia Episcopal Theological Seminary in Alexandria, Virginia, in 1952. Virginia Seminary had a national reputation for being "low church" Episcopalian: The Virginia Seminary student was taught that Sunday morning services consisted of the simpler service of Morning Prayer rather than the Celebration of the Holy Eucharist. Low churchmanship meant that liturgical flourish was kept to a minimum; there were no candlesticks on the altar or reserved sacrament in a tabernacle on the altar or wall. Outside of church, a shirt, suit, and tie were clerical garb for low church clergy, rather than the black shirt and white clerical collar. When addressed in writing, the "low church" priest would be "the Reverend Mr." and when met on the street, the priest was to be greeted by his last name preceded by the title "Mister"; the high church Anglo-Catholic title, Father, is almost never heard in low church circles. In all of this, the Rev. Philip Gresham was not the typical Virginia

Rev. Philip M. Gresham

Seminary graduate. It is difficult to find a picture of Gresham where he is not wearing a black clergy shirt with a high and highly starched Anglican collar, and as Christ Church would find out, Philip Gresham loved liturgy in all of its forms.

In June of 1952, Gresham was ordained to the priesthood in the Diocese of Virginia. The young cleric was made priest-in-charge of the Mission Home District of Neve Parish Archdeaconry of the Blue Ridge,[44] with missionary work in the mountain areas of Greene and Albemarle counties. On February 14, 1954, Gresham took up the position of associate rector at St. James Episcopal Church in Richmond, one of the oldest and most prestigious churches in Virginia.[45] As part of his varied duties as associate rector of St. James, according to one newspaper source, Gresham during this time taught Sacred Studies at St. Christopher's School and was also coach of the wrestling team.[46]

When the call came from Christ Church in Martinsville in the summer of 1956, Gresham was initially reluctant to leave his position under the Rev. Churchill J. Gibson.[47] Gresham's departure would leave an opening that Gibson would need to fill. For Gibson, who had served his parish since 1929 and was scheduled to retire in April of 1957, this would be a difficult recruitment. Associates serve at the pleasure of the rector and Gibson would be hard pressed to find a qualified priest willing to make a move for a position with an expected short life span. It was typical of Gresham to feel loyalty to his rector and not want to leave him in a difficult position. Gresham would show this type of loyalty and deference to the needs of others again and again over the years. He wrestled with the idea of refusing the call to prestigious Christ Church in order to remain at St. James until his rector's retirement. He decided he would not leave without his rector's consent. Gibson must have given the young priest his blessing to take the position in Martinsville because on September 2, 1956, it was announced at services at Christ Church that their new rector would be the Rev. Philip M. Gresham.[48]

Like a bride before her wedding—as the consummation of their search approached—the members of Christ Church could hardly wait for the day of Philip Gresham's arrival. The congregation made every effort to make their new priest feel welcomed in Martinsville. In the Sunday Bulletin for September 9, 1956, it was announced that "Mr. Gresham will preach his first Sermon here on October 14, according to his present plans."[49] For their part, the vestry planned a private party, limited to the vestry members, their wives and Gresham, for Monday evening September 17 at Justice Whittle's home.[50] The vestry also voted "that the church should equip the rector's office, i.e., cost of equipping the office to be borne by the parish." Gresham requested that some help be given to him to furnish the rectory's study and living room. After meeting with the Executive Board of the Church's Women's Auxiliary, its Project committee and the vestry, it was agreed that Gresham could purchase furniture estimated to cost $950.00 with the understanding "that on behalf of the parish, the vestry, and the Auxiliary will underwrite the cost but with no commitment upon the Auxiliary as to any definite share."[51]

The excitement grew as the day for Gresham's inaugural service approached. Christ Church member Ann Gardner recalls that the new 29-year-old rector was "full of enthusiasm and energy"[52] that set him apart from the former rector. The Rev. Dr. Charles Fishburne lived a few doors down from Gardner. She was best friends with Fishburne's daughter and remembers Fishburne as a "father figure, a delightful, sweet man…a quiet, low key person that everybody liked." When recalling the contrast between Fishburne and Gresham,

Gardner says, "It was the difference between Ike Eisenhower and John F. Kennedy with Gresham being Kennedy."

A new rector at Christ Episcopal Church touched more than just its congregation; it was an event felt by the entire Martinsville community. The local newspaper, the *Martinsville News Bulletin,* kept its readers informed about Gresham's call and about his first services at Christ Church's altar. For Gresham Sunday morning, October 14, began at 8 a.m. with a quiet celebration of the Holy Eucharist with the few members not willing to wait to see their new priest in action at the principal service. There followed the routine church school from 9:30 a.m. to 10:30 a.m. and, as usual, M. E. Whitner Jr. led the Bible class for adults. Then, at 11:00 a.m., the organ swelled inside a packed church nave as the congregation sang the opening hymn, #266, "Holy, Holy, Holy! Lord God Almighty! Early in the morning our song shall rise to thee."[53] As the congregation stood to sing, most people in the pews had to crane their necks to get their first glimpse of their new young, handsome, solidly built, and unexpectedly short priest. Even the three teenage acolytes who led the procession, John Swezey, Duke Sutton, and Charles Cole, stood taller than their rector. Prior to the service, a Coca-Cola crate had been quietly placed behind the pulpit for Gresham to stand on, lest the preacher not be able to see his congregation or they him. Also, a week prior to the service, the incoming rector exercised his new-found prerogative as chief liturgist of the congregation and declined to use the readings assigned for that Sunday, the Twentieth Sunday after Trinity, by the 1928 Book of Common Prayer. Instead, Gresham chose to read the Gospel from Matthew 6:1–15, the verses where Jesus teaches his disciples to pray the Lord's Prayer. The sermon that Gresham preached was entitled, "Confirming on Feeble Knees," a reference to the first lesson read that morning from the 35th chapter of Isaiah, verse 3, "Strengthen ye the weak hands, and confirm the feeble knees." Sadly, there are no known copies of this or any of Gresham's sermons.

Gresham's first Sunday Bulletin gave an early hint to the liturgical leanings of the new rector in a bold way. He announced that the early service at 8 a.m. would be a Communion Service each Sunday. During Charles Fishburne's nearly 20-year rectorship, the earlier Sunday service had been Morning Prayer. Attempting to change the liturgical habits of Episcopalians is no small thing and I am sure that the 8 o'clockers would have something to say about the switch in service, but not on this day. This was a Sunday for celebration. Also, the Bulletin announced that there would be "a reception for the Rev. Mr. Gresham" on October 17 given by the Woman's Auxiliary. Most of the congregation was already aware of the reception because the ladies had sent out engraved invitations that read, "The Woman's Auxiliary of Christ Episcopal Church Request your presence at a reception in Honor of The Rev. Phillip Morton Gresham in the Church School Auditorium on Wednesday evening, October 17 at eight o'clock." It is assumed that they learned quickly that Gresham spelled his first name, Philip, with only one "l".

Despite the typo on the invitation, "approximately 150 members of the congregation, local ministers and their wives, and additional guests" attended.[54] The new rector of Christ Episcopal Church had immediate cachet in Martinsville. "In the receiving line with the new rector were the Senior Warden, Justice Whittle, and his wife; the Junior Warden and Martinsville Mayor, Fred Woodson, and his wife; and the church Treasurer, Clarence P. Kearfott and his wife"—who was the current president of the Woman's Auxiliary. As was fitting for such an event, the *Martinsville News Bulletin* reported, the "silver appointments were used on the serving table at each end of the church parish hall where centerpieces of chrysanthemums in bold autumn colors were flanked by silver candelabra holding lighted tapers."

By the end of his first week, the Rev. Philip M. Gresham had every reason to believe that he had found a home in Martinsville for the next 10 to 20 years. His predecessor, the Rev. Dr. Fishburne, had lasted two decades, and Gresham could have every expectation to match that record. Gresham was widely hailed as being intelligent, enthusiastic, and personable—just the combination of characteristics that make for a successful long-term tenure as pastor of a congregation. What he lacked were years of practical experience as sole priest in charge. He would soon find that he was rector of a congregation filled with more than its share of dominant personalities, entering a time of national cultural upheaval. The young priest had risen far above many of his age and experience. It was yet to be seen how long his rise could continue.

7

Legacy of Guilt

If marriage is the metaphor, churches love when considering the relationship between the clergy and the congregation, then they must also admit that, as in many marriages, there can be conflict and even dysfunction in the family, especially when it comes to race.

Less than four months after his "I have a Dream" speech on the Washington, DC, Mall, the Reverend Martin Luther King Jr. made the oft-quoted observation that "We must face the fact that in America, the church is still the most segregated major institution in America. At 11:00 on Sunday morning when we stand and sing Christ has no east or west, we stand at the most segregated hour in this nation."[55] King's pronouncement on this lamentable state of Christianity is still applicable today; it was certainly operative for those years in which Father Gresham, his vestry, and his bishop would face irreconcilable differences over their deeply segregated church and community.

There is plenty of guilt to live down in the Episcopal Church, not least its stance on slavery in the 19th century. While almost every other denomination in America wrestled with the greatest moral question of the century, many of them fracturing over it, the Episcopal Church chose mostly to ignore it. While Methodists,

Baptists, and Presbyterians divided north and south over the issue of slavery, Episcopalians clung cravenly to institutional unity. During the Civil War, the Episcopal Church's General Convention, seemingly deaf to the conflict, marked the bishops and deputies from dioceses in the Confederate States absent. Meanwhile, Bishop Leonidas Polk of Louisiana "strapped sword over robe" and died on the battlefield as a Confederate general. When the war ended, the Episcopal dioceses of the old Confederacy were once again marked as present at the General Convention as if nothing unusual had taken place in the years since they last attended. Christ Episcopal Church would, years later, include in its list of rectors the notorious military scout and spy, Frank Stringfellow, once labeled as "the most dangerous man in the Confederacy" with a $10,000.00 bounty on his head.[56]

The archives of The Episcopal Church make the straightforward assessment that the Civil War changed little in the church for African-American Episcopalians; they were still separate and unequal. In 1878, a separate seminary was formed by Virginia Theological Seminary to educate black priests. Increasingly, black priests pushed to be included for consideration as bishops. The first two black bishops, James Theodore Holly, consecrated in 1874 as Bishop of Haiti, and Samuel David Ferguson, consecrated as Bishop of Liberia in 1885, were celebrated as pioneers for black Episcopalians, albeit as bishops for dioceses where there were no white candidates. It was not until 1917 that the Diocese of Arkansas elected a black suffragan bishop as assistant bishop to the white diocesan bishop. Still, these black bishops, like black priests and black deacons, were limited to "Colored work."[57] In 1886, the Conference of Church Workers Among Colored People was formed to push for the full inclusion of blacks in the life of the church.[58] It is an inescapable conclusion that for most of its history, as even the church's own archives admit, "the Episcopal Church treated African-Americans as a problem: culturally and socially separated and inferior, but by baptism, full and equal members of the community."[59]

In Martinsville in the 1940s, the diocese addressed the perceived problem of African-American Episcopalians by accepting the application for an all-black congregation, St. Paul's Episcopal Church. In October 1940, a petition for the new church had been presented to Bishop Henry D. Phillips by Dr. L. A. Vickers, a distinguished black dentist in Martinsville.[60] The next month a group of fourteen African-Americans met with Bishop Phillips at the home of a notable civic leader in the black community, Dr. Harry Williams, where Vickers offered to start a Bible class under the direction of the Christ Church rector, the Rev. Charles Fishburne. Thirteen months later, seventeen candidates from St. Paul's Church were presented to the bishop for the sacrament of Confirmation at a service held at the Henry County Training Center on West Fayette Street in Martinsville. It is worth noting and a sad commentary on the times that the confirmation of these African-American candidates did not take place in a church, although Episcopal confirmation services typically do. There is no record of that option even being raised.

Beginning in 1941, regular services were held for the small congregation in the home of African-American school teacher Mary E. McDaniel on East Church Street, less than a mile from Christ Church. In 1948, services were moved to St. Paul's current site on the west side of Martinsville, where the congregation had finished the basement on property donated by Dr. Vickers. Services and Sunday school continued in the undercroft until May of 1955 when the nave of the church was completed. In the 1950s, the church was the location of the first free preschool for black children. While never a large church, St. Paul's membership included many of the influential black business and community leaders in Martinsville. "Small but prominent in the black community" could describe all five of the African-American Episcopal churches in the Diocese of Southwestern Virginia during this period.[61]

The moment Philip Gresham stepped into the pulpit at Christ Church in 1956, he took on the mantles of both a community leader and a religious leader. In the community and in the church, the racial lines had been clearly drawn, and the movers and shakers of Martinsville—who were also the movers and shakers of Christ Church—saw no reason to disturb them. Attitudes toward race had begun to evolve among the leadership of the Episcopal Church, especially among the clergy, but the change was slow and irresolute. As rector of a prominent Episcopal church, Gresham was in a position to make a difference, if he cared to play that role.

As thoughtful and informed priest, Gresham would have been well aware of the historic struggle for racial equality that was playing out on much larger stages, and within the church itself, throughout the South. In 1951, the School of Theology at the University of the South in Sewanee, Tennessee, an institution owned and governed by 28 dioceses of the southeastern United States founded in 1858, was directed to integrate by vote of its Provincial Synod. When the Board of Trustees of the University refused the resolution to integrate the school, most of the seminary's faculty resigned in protest.[62] Sewanee, as the University of the South is commonly known, is a small school with an outsized reputation, and this conflict between the University and the seminary reverberated throughout the church so strongly that the Board was forced to reverse its decision in 1953. It is certain that the Board felt pressured by the General Convention of the Episcopal Church that met in 1952 and voted a resolution stating, "[W]e consistently oppose and combat discrimination based on color or race in every form, both within the church and without, in this country and internationally." In passing, it should be noted that the University of the South's policy dispute over the admission of black students concerned only black male students; the gender barrier was not breached at Sewanee until 1969.[63]

In 1958, only 125 of the Diocese of Southwestern Virginia's 9,700 communicants were African-American, but the campaign for their inclusion in all church events without racial separation would tear at the soul of the Episcopal Church throughout the diocese. The battleground for this struggle would be a Camp & Conference Center outside of Marion, Virginia, named Hemlock Haven. It would fall largely on the bishop of the diocese, William Henry Marmion, to hold his diocese together in an increasingly bitter racial divide. Christ Church would have a central role to play, and its rector would be swept up in the struggle, but not before the young priest had made an indelible mark in the hearts of many parishioners.[64]

8

Hemlock Haven

In the early 1950s, the Right Reverend William Marmion must have felt that there was nothing better than being Bishop of Southwest Virginia. Bishops, of course, have their honeymoon period just as surely as rectors do. But then, once a year, the bishop must face the reality of dealing, not with the happy sheep of his flock, but with the Diocesan Council, the ecclesiastical version of a shareholders meeting of the not-for-profit corporation that is the diocese. To the Council, each parish and mission sends a number of delegates elected by their respective congregations, the number determined by the size of the church, to a meeting that will elect officers, manage the finances, and pass legislation for the functioning of the diocese. As most bishops and delegates will tell you, these meetings are reminiscent of the nursery rhyme about "the little girl who had a little curl, right in the middle of her forehead, who when she was good was very, very good, but when she was bad, she was horrid." Bishop Marmion would become well acquainted with this "little girl" over the years of Diocesan Council meetings. But at his early council meetings, the little girl was well behaved as the bishop laid out a bold plan for a conference center.

At the annual Council for the Diocese of Southwestern Virginia in 1955, Bishop Marmion used the Bishop's Address, a diocesan bishop's version of the State of the Union address, to prepare his people for what was in store once they acquired a camp and conference center. As recorded in the 1955 Journal of the Diocese, he began by commending the work of the committee on the Diocesan Camp and Conference Center for its work during the past year, noting that while he had nothing yet to show the Council for their work, the committee, he quipped, had "traveled far and wide and knows lots of places that are unsuitable."[65]

Then, after a few words about the diocesan survey that would begin later that year, Marmion took up the issue of race relations in the diocese. He began with an international reference to the Anglican Congress meeting from the past August, where "a resolution was passed to the effect that people of all races and cultures should be welcome to attend any service of any church in the Anglican Communion." He reminded the Council that this was similar to the stand taken at various times by the Episcopal General Convention and by the House of Bishops.

Marmion was blunt about current behavior not rising to the standard of being a welcoming church. "Obviously," he said, "we have much to do by way of implementing these sentiments on the diocesan and local levels." As for the future in the diocese, meetings were to be racially mixed and the diocese would work to find venues in Virginia where such meetings could occur. "We are going out of our way to find places for convocational and diocesan meetings where there is no discrimination against our Colored brethren," he continued. And, just in case there was any doubt in anyone's mind about where the bishop stood on the policy of racial integration in the diocese, he then made it abundantly clear. "The official policy of the diocese at such meetings is to make no distinction because of race or color." Marmion was aware that policy alone would not change long-standing prejudices for either blacks or whites. "All of us stand under God's judgment," he said. The few African-American delegates to Council were gently admonished by their bishop to cooperate in this difficult enterprise: "Sometimes we have difficulty getting our Colored brethren to cooperate after we have gone to great lengths to make it possible for them to experience full fellowship with us."

Marmion concluded his remarks on race relations by reporting that the National Council of the Episcopal Church took up the "Supreme Court's decision which established the illegality of segregation in our public schools." The result was a study document for the church entitled "Just, Right and Necessary." Then, at the National Council's regular quarterly meeting the past December, Council delegates had "unanimously passed a resolution affirming the justice of the Court's decision from the point of view of Christian Morals, as well as from the point of view of law and democratic principles."

As he toured the diocese on his regularly scheduled episcopal visits, at each stop Marmion championed the need for a diocesan camp and conference center. In most Episcopal churches on the occasion of a visit from their bishop, a special meeting of the vestry is called so that the leader of the diocese and the leaders of the local congregation can report to each other, ask and answer questions. Philip Gresham had only been rector of Christ Church for a few months when Marmion made his annual visitation to Christ Church on October 27, 1956. Since Gresham was still new in his job, it fell to the senior warden, Justice Whittle, to present a report covering "both temporal and spiritual activities of the parish during the year, comparing same with those of 1955."[66] For his part, Marmion ran through the various diocesan activities that would be of interest to parishioners in Martinsville. Reminding the vestry that Christ Church was one of two congregations in town, the bishop spent some time on the "status of the four Negro parishes of the diocese," which would have included St. Paul's Church on Fayette Street. Marmion then concluded his remarks to the vestry with a pitch for support of a diocesan camp and conference center.

While there is no official designation, everyone in a diocese knows which are the cardinal parishes—those that because of their size and wealth are preeminent among their peers in prestige and influence. In Southwest Virginia, Christ Church was known as such, and as one of the cardinal parishes of the diocese, was represented on most of the important diocesan committees, the Camp and Conference Center Committee being no exception. For that important seat, Christ Church vestryman Clarence H. Burrage was given the honor. Burrage dutifully detailed to the parish vestry what was happening at each step of the way with this diocesan priority. On April 2, 1957, Burrage must have been thrilled to report that the Camp and Conference Center Committee was about to select a "site located near the Blue Ridge Parkway some nine miles south of Adney Gap, which when acquired and developed, will be ideal for its purpose."[67] The exact location of this property is difficult to determine from this description, but he may have been referring to the area that is the present-day Phoebe Needles Center. The Phoebe Needles Center was already owned by the diocese and had been used over the years as a school and center for mission. While it might need developing, it would not need to be acquired. Regardless of its exact location, the placement of the Diocesan Camp and Conference Center near Adney Gap would locate it approximately 50 miles from Martinsville, making the camp even more of an asset for the congregation because of its proximity. Evidently, the Adney Gap location proved to be a false alarm. At a June 5 vestry meeting, Burrage reported that the diocesan committee was continuing to study "available sites," describing several of them for his fellow vestry members.[68]

Things must have moved quickly for the diocesan site selection committee, because at the vestry meeting on July 3, 1957, Burrage reported that the committee had selected a "certain already-developed property," Hemlock Haven.[69] Absent from this announcement was the thrill experienced in April. Although situated in a beautiful location adjacent to Hungry Mother State Park and Jefferson National Forest, Hemlock Haven would be a two-and-a-half-hour drive from Martinsville. At the August vestry meeting, Burrage reported that the diocese had closed the deal for Hemlock Haven for "the sum of $55,000.00."[70] The Diocese of Southwestern Virginia had a Camp and Conference Center to call its own. No longer would it struggle to find a conference venue that would welcome all diocesan participants, black and white, for its events. In September, Burrage informed the vestry that the new conference center was already being used for a diocesan clergy conference and that the Hemlock Haven property would be designated "Camp Phillips in honor of the late Bishop Phillips."[71] Given the future controversy surrounding the Diocesan Camp and Conference Center, I am confident that Bishop Phillips, were he still alive, would not be unhappy that almost no one ever referred to Hemlock Haven using his name. Still, with the purchase of Hemlock Haven, Bishop Marmion and his diocese could, at least for the moment, breathe the fresh, sweet air of success.

9

"The Best Priest Ever"

It is rare and therefore a matter of intense pride for a church to have a bishop as part of its lineage. At Christ Episcopal Church in Martinsville, the wall of rectors' portraits includes a number of priests with impressive resumes; two of them would become bishops. On my first tour of that wall, I was surprised to find a picture of the Rev. James Coleman. Shortly before he became the Bishop of West Tennessee, Coleman was one of the priests in the Diocese of Louisiana who interviewed me as an aspirant for Holy Orders. And here he was in Martinsville, a part of his history of which I'd been unaware. Also on the wall was a picture of the Rev. George Packard, a decorated Vietnam veteran who became Bishop for the United States Armed Forces. With such a stellar heritage of talent, rectors of Christ Episcopal Church begin their ministry with a cache of formidable influence in the church locally and nationally. Great priests served Christ Church over its nearly two centuries of existence. Yet the one priest who captured the hearts and memories of so many long-time members, the name that is repeated as "the best priest ever," is Phil Gresham.

To the youth of Christ Church, Gresham was a rock star. To their parents, the young, energetic priest was just what the vibrant town of Martinsville needed. I cannot imagine that Gresham was not filled with the exuberance of the good feelings that surrounded him. Was there anything better than being the rector of Christ Episcopal Church in Martinsville, Virginia, in the late 1950s? Gresham would drive his powder-blue Thunderbird convertible through an area that was growing and prosperous. Martinsville was home to the largest nylon factory in the world. The region was home to major furniture companies. Just outside of Martinsville, Chicago's Marshall Field department store built a textile factory to supply its stores with linens and towels and then developed an entire town to house the factory's workers. On a pleasant day, Gresham could retract the roof on the T-Bird and cruise the mountain roads just outside of town. An hour's drive along the Blue Ridge Parkway could restore a soul faster than a three-day religious retreat; a hike through the forest of Fairy Stone Park could revitalize the spirit as quickly as priestly absolution.

If Gresham felt like a swim on a hot day it was a short drive or a long walk from Christ Church's rectory to one of Martinsville's unique landmarks, the Liberty Heights Swimming pool owned by the Lester Lumber Company. When local businessman G. T. Lester lost two lumber mills to fire in the space of three years, he was determined to devise a scheme to prevent a repeat of the catastrophes.[72] For the Jones Creek plant at the edge of town, Lester rebuilt the facility with what must have seemed foolproof fire protection. On the hill overlooking the plant he built a two-million-gallon reservoir, a ready source of water for any fire in the factory below. As a service to the community, the reservoir doubled as a community swimming pool that could accommodate up to two thousand swimmers. The pool was divided into three circular sections: an 18-inch-deep wading pool on the outside, separated by a wall from a four-foot-deep middle section, with a 12-foot-deep section at the center.[73] The deepest section included three diving platforms of varying heights. Opened in the summer of 1926, the Liberty Heights Swimming pool was a fabulous success. Over the years, it added locker rooms for swimmers, a refreshment stand that rented out skates when the covered pavilion was not being used for dances, and a deck for sunbathing, a diversion that was just coming into style.

Gresham would have arrived in Martinsville too late to know the glory days of the Liberty Heights swimming pool. As the city continued to prosper, privately owned pools and private clubs with pools were attracting Martinsville swimmers. With its popularity fading, the Jones Creek plant's fire protection reservoir ceased operating as the community pool in 1957.

But the Lester family's innovation was just one instance of the many ways Martinsville prospered and enjoyed its communal prosperity. By the mid-50s, the post-war boom was booming around Christ Church. There was an economic boom, a baby boom, a technological boom, and even a religious boom. Society's high regard for religion in the 1950s meant that respectable people were expected to be in church; Sunday "blue laws" restricted shopping and other activities, reducing the distractions for churchgoers. At a time when most people were genuinely devoted to their denomination and interested in religious topics, the young rector of Christ Church was in demand from the moment he arrived in Martinsville.

On the Sunday of Gresham's installation as rector, the pew sheet for the service included an announcement informing the congregation that "Your rector is to be away next Sunday. He will be preaching at Sweet Briar and Hollins College."[74] The local paper covered the engagement at Sweet Briar College under the header "Gresham Believes Man's Soul Sick."[75] Using Danish philosopher Soren Kierkegaard's understanding of human anxiety causing a "sickness unto death," Gresham told his college audience that the sickness of our times is "despair and its kinsmen—boredom, restlessness, and insecurity." Noting that the average person in the pew would have trouble defining what he means by soul, Gresham went on to say, "man's spirit is what integrates his mind and body, coordinating them into a healthy functioning unit. And as man can be healthy or sick in mind or body, he similarly can be healthy or sick in spirit." Already in this early sermon at Sweet Briar, the newly minted rector was wrestling with the belief that "perhaps the sickness of our comfortable twentieth century is one of the soul."

The newspaper's very brief description of Gresham's remarks at Sweet Briar is one of the few accounts of Gresham's preaching. It is possible that even this example may not be typical of Gresham's style, since this sermon was delivered to a congregation made up of college students and faculty rather than families in a parish. A good preacher will conform the intricacy of a presentation to the capacity of the audience, and that is probably what Gresham was doing here. A disappointing shortcoming of Christ Episcopal Church's archives is that no copies of Gresham's sermons are on file. Still, the direction he took that Sunday at Sweet Briar is indicative of the young, parish priest whose nimble mind could move comfortably from a pulpit in a family church to quoting controversial and cutting-edge existentialism at a college chapel. A mental and spiritual ability that was especially cherished by Gresham's younger admirers in Martinsville.

Christ Church's rector's reputation as a noteworthy speaker grew with each new invitation to speak. During Lent in 1957, Gresham gave a series of eleven radio broadcasts on the "Episcopal Hour" for local Martinsville station WMVA. The vestry helped to sponsor the series on behalf of Christ Church at a cost of $165.00. Since this was an unbudgeted expense, the vestry minutes show that the vestry also voted to pay for the radio sponsorship by "reappropriating the $25.00 per month originally earmarked as choir director's salary to meet the costs of a series of Lenten radio broadcasts (during 1957) to be conducted by the rector, who is serving without pay as choir director."[76] Gresham's speaking engagements were wide-ranging. The *Martinsville Bulletin* ran an article on February 22, 1957, under the heading "Episcopal Rector to Address Synagogue Sabbath Eve Meeting." Gresham was the principal speaker at Ohev Zion Synagogue for the annual observance of National Brotherhood Week. Again, there are no transcripts of his presentation other than the topic, which was "A Case of Growing Together."

Gresham was widely acclaimed as a captivating speaker. It is disheartening that the only record of his speeches or sermons are snippets from newspaper articles with the usual degree of uncertainty about the accuracy of what he said and scant account of how he said it. We know that Gresham spoke in Floyd, Virginia, to the Floyd Court House Women's Club. The local paper ran a brief column under the heading, "Rev. Philip Gresham Addresses Floyd Group."[77] The tantalizing topic for the night was "The Power of the Personal," but all we know of what was said was the paper's brief report that Gresham spoke about the middle years of life, "defined as the period after the completion of preparation for life to the retirement from living." He said that many people find life as a process of getting into ruts and that "people need not to be trapped in the rush [sic] because the middle years is the greatest period to develop the power of the personal." The article went on to say that "Rev. Mr. Gresham listed several ways to cultivate this power. To understand instead of judging; to develop the power of listening; to be one's real self; to accept hostility, and to develop some creative interests." It is truly sad that all we know of what Gresham said in Floyd that day is one rather brief news clip.

Gresham was most popular as a youth leader. Often, he had a leadership role at youth events in his own church, in the diocese, and in the community. The Sunday edition of the *Martinsville Bulletin* for May 28, 1957, ran a picture of Gresham, the baccalaureate preacher that year, under the banner, "Martinsville High sets Graduation Exercises." Gresham would find out that graduation at Martinsville High School was steeped in tradition. On the Friday prior to commencements, there would be the annual senior assembly, the final assembly of the school year and, for the graduates, the last assembly at their high school. The entire school would gather in the auditorium, each class seated together.[78] All year, every year, the best seats in the front were reserved for the senior class; the juniors sat behind them, sophomores behind the juniors, the freshmen class relegated to the back of the hall, and the eighth graders consigned to sit in the balcony.

Gresham with acolytes

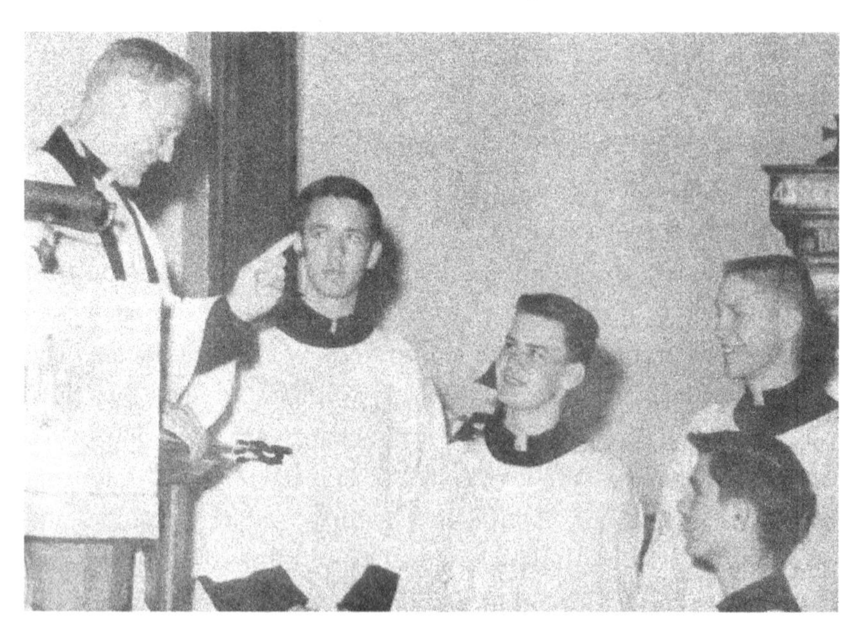

After an eternity of quasi-attentiveness to announcements, reminiscences of a wonderful school year and congratulations to the graduating students, the senior class rose from their seats and marched out of the auditorium. The juniors would then rise and take the seats left to them by the graduating class. Each class in turn advanced to the seats left to them by the class in front of them. Once both spatially and metaphorically promoted, the Martinsville students would hear the final dismissal for the school year.

Then, on the Sunday evening before commencement exercises, the graduates, with their families and friends, would fill the high school auditorium for the baccalaureate service. The *Martinsville Bulletin* would report that "500 parents, students and faculty attended" the 1957 baccalaureate, where the seniors marched "solemnly into the auditorium" to the hymn "God of Our Fathers." The *Bulletin* went on to report that Gresham "gave an excellent sermon." In the opinion of 1960 Martinsville High school graduate John Swezey, most baccalaureate sermons are forgettable for their repetition. Gresham's homily was different. Swezey recalls, "Philip loved sarcasm. When graduation speakers all say, 'You have the world in your hands, you are the future, you will be this and that,' Philip said, 'You have the world, you are the future, you will have all of these opportunities; you will have the world in your hands and...it will want to crush you!'" Gresham's unexpectedly candid remarks brought sustained laughter and applause from the senior class, if not their teachers and family. But this connection with the youth is exactly why Gresham had such a loyal following.

Ann Gardner was one of those young people excited by the arrival of the new priest. Although she had been baptized by Gresham's predecessor, Charles Fishburne, and was best friends with Fishburne's daughter, she remembers being ready for the changes Gresham's youthful energy inspired. Fishburne was a "father figure" who preferred everything "regimented and the same." Things were different once Gresham arrived. Gardner recalls, "You know how people resist change; everybody is comfortable when things are the same...Then, all of a sudden, here comes this young man who wants to do this and wants to do that...I mean it was great because we were waiting for someone like him. And the way the youth gravitated towards him! We were just waiting for someone like him. All the teachers were older than the hills, all the Sunday school teachers were older than the hills, the minister was older than the hills and here comes this guy who looks like he's just out of high school, like he's one of us! It was like 'Let's go get the world and do something with it!'"[79]

Change things he did, and they loved Gresham for it. At the 1958 Annual Congregational Meeting, Ruth Drewry, president of the Christ Church Youth League, reported on activities for the preceding year. In her remarks, she offered thanks for the "Juke Box from Mr. Leonard Gardner" and for the "Pool table from Mrs. Covington, brought with the help of Mr. Al Mays and Mr. Wooldridge." To most students and parents today, a church youth room with a pool table and music would hardly be noticed, even less a cause for concern. But this was 1957, the same year that *Music Man* hit Broadway. In that fabulously successful musical, Professor Harold Hill warns the parents of River City of the "trouble, with a capital T" that would come when their children start shooting pool. Before the parents of Martinsville could face the "trouble" prophesied by Professor Hill, circumstances intervened. Christ Church's youth never got the chance to shoot any stick on Christ Church's pool table. It was the architecture of the building, not the civic virtue of the people that kept the pool balls unracked. In a classic example of unintended consequences, Mrs. Covington's donation was overly generous. The pool table was of the highest quality, with a heavy marble top and heavy carved side rails and legs. This elegant and very heavy pool table was intended as a centerpiece of the youth room in the basement of the church. However, the basement sat atop of a sub-basement. The vestry was advised that the floor of the undercroft might not support the additional weight safely.[80] Using church funds to reinforce the floor so the youth could hang out and shoot pool was, to say the least, unlikely. The pool table was relegated to storage in the sub-basement until a plan could be worked out for its setup, a task the vestry assigned to its property committee.[81] No plan was ever proposed, and no one has any memory of whatever became of the Youth Group's pool table.

The jukebox was a different story with a happier ending; all of Gresham's youth fondly remember it. The story of the jukebox has an unusual genesis. It begins when Gresham intervened with a man struggling with alcoholism. At the time, Leonard Gardner was a member of another church in town.[82] As often happens in these situations, Gardner preferred not to acknowledge his problem to his pastor and risk the embarrassment of his condition becoming known in his own congregation. Instead, Gardner sought out a respected member of the clergy from a church not his own, the rector of Christ Church. Whether they met just once or multiple times, Gresham's advice to Gardner must have been successful. In appreciation for the help he received, Gardner, who owned an amusement company that sold juke boxes, pinball machines, and soda dispensers, offered a jukebox to Christ Church's youth group. No one complained that the jukebox was filled with old technology, 78 rpm records. According to John Swezey, the jukebox made Christ Episcopal Church "the scandal of the town, because those Episcopalians had that jukebox and they danced on Sunday nights in the church."[83] He added with a smile, "And that is why our youth group would have fifty students show up every week, because we danced on Sunday nights in the church!"

For high school students, Christ Church became the place in town to hang out and its rector was a hero to the local youth, Episcopalian or not. Gresham was especially popular with the teenage boys because of his wrestling prowess. When the former college wrestler learned that Martinsville High School did not have a wrestling team, he volunteered his time to form a wrestling club for the students. Martinsville High School was a few blocks from the church and rectory, easy access for the priest. Gresham worked with the school administration to provide space for a wrestling team. Across the street from the high school on Cleveland Street stood the derelict old Central Grammar School building. On the first floor there was a weight room with old gymnastic mats that the school lent to Gresham's wrestling club for practice. As Swezey recalls, "We wrestled in grey shorts that one of the Pannill people donated to us and tee-shirts that had 'Martinsville High School' emblazoned on the front. That was our uniform." To promote the club and to recruit wrestlers, Gresham put on exhibition matches. Swezey remembers his participation in one such exhibition match with Barry Greene. The competition was vigorous between the two boys, both wrestling at their high school weight of 150 pounds. To the delight of the crowd the two boys threw each other around the mats for several minutes. Ultimately, the match was halted by Gresham when he realized that the two newbie wrestlers were so evenly matched and limited in wrestling experience that neither was getting any advantage over the other and both were nearing exhaustion.

The wrestling exhibition matches proved successful in attracting high school boys to the sport. Once he was able to fill a roster with wrestlers, Gresham was able to schedule matches with other schools. One of their first bouts was with the wrestling team from the small rural high school in the town of Climax.

In the late 1950s, Martinsville High School Bulldogs were a sports powerhouse. The varsity football team of 1958 won seven games with one tie and one loss; six of the seven wins were shutouts.[84] As proof that the 1958 winning season was not just a fluke, the 1960 varsity football team had eight wins, one tie and one loss, and seven of the eight wins were shutouts.[85] The Martinsville baseball and track teams were equally formidable with similar winning records. There was every reason to expect the Martinsville High wrestling team would live up to the school's victorious tradition. Every wrestler who boarded the team bus with "coach" Gresham for the trip to Climax High School expected to return to Martinsville a winner.[86]

Nobody on the "Bulldog Bus" was quite sure which was the best road to take to Climax or exactly where in town the Climax high school stood. The bus bounced and swayed as it wound its way for thirty minutes over country roads. The stiff bus springs coiled and released with every bump and turn sending the wrestlers ricocheting off walls and ceiling inside. Despite the beating of the ride over, the MAVAHI wrestlers were in high spirits when they finally arrived at the small gym next to Climax High School. The athletes made their way to the locker room for visiting teams and changed into their grey shorts and tee shirts proudly emblazoned with Martinsville High School lettering. After a few words of encouragement from Coach Gresham, their game faces on, the Martinsville Wrestling team strutted its way into the bright lights of the gym.

Nothing had prepared them for what opened up in front of them. Instead of the worn, rough, dusty old tumbling mats they practiced on in the rundown Central Grammar school building, the floor of the Climax gym was covered in new, padded wrestling mats with the official regulation twenty-eight-foot circular wrestling area surrounding a ten-foot circle that enclosed an arrow to position the wrestlers for the start of each match. Still more surprising to the Martinsville wrestlers was the attendance for the competition. Every space in the gym's bleachers was filled with students and families from the Climax community.

As the Martinsville team entered, the wrestling referee pointed to the visitor's bench and Gresham led his astounded wrestlers to their area to await the entrance of the home team. The indistinct murmuring of the crowd broke into thunderous applause, whistles, and whoops when the door to the home team locker room burst open and out marched the Climax wrestling team. Each boy was wearing an official wrestler's one-piece singlet with heel-less regulation wrestler's shoes. A few of the larger wrestlers wore full length tights with stirrups under their singlets. The home team marched in front of the packed stands on either side of the small gym and then lined up across the mats in rows. In perfectly coordinated maneuvers, the line of boys began a practiced routine of calisthenics designed to feature the strength and agility of the athletes and to bring the crowd to its feet. As the home team finished their display of one-armed pushups, it dawned on Gresham that he did not see a football stadium or baseball field at Climax High School. It was the wrestling team that was the pride of the Climax athletics program. These boys were all tanned and muscled from days of working on their family farms. Years of experience as a wrestler and a coach made Gresham realize that this was going to be a long evening.

Actually, it wasn't as long an evening as Gresham feared; few of the bouts lasted more than a minute or two, with each of his wrestlers being pinned to the mat in relatively short order. At 170 pounds, Charlie Cole was wrestling as a heavyweight in the last match of the night.[87] Gresham pulled Charlie to the side before his bout and they both took a knee. Calling up all of his best Knute Rockne inspiration, Coach Gresham told Charlie he was the one last, best hope that his team would not return to Martinsville without a single victory. Then, Gresham the coach became Gresham the priest and prayerfully invoked the power of heaven to carry Cole into the winner's circle. Cole gave a confident, "Amen." Thirty seconds later, Cole was pinned to the mat by the Climax heavyweight. Martinsville was shut out.

On the ride home, one of the boys informed Gresham that it would be better for the wrestlers the next day at school if they all agreed that the tournament at Climax never took place. They were all willing to agree to say that the bus got lost on the ride to Climax and they had to forfeit their matches. Tempting though the offer was for the wrestling coach, the priest, albeit reluctantly, had to say no. As President Theodore Roosevelt could have told Gresham and his team about their experiences at Climax, "At the worst, if he fails, at least he fails while daring greatly." The "greatest priest" would have to learn to live with some defeats.

10

Bishop William Henry Marmion

Gresham's refusal to lie about the Climax wrestling match may not have taken the moral courage of Martin Luther at the Diet of Worms, but it served as a moral lesson for the high school wrestling team at a time when what was moral and what was legal were rapidly becoming a hot topic, especially around race and civil rights. It was a time when it was perfectly legal to refuse to serve a black person at a lunch counter reserved for whites. There was a growing chorus in the 1950s of people who objected to this bias for legality over morality.

There were always those who recognized moral imperative and acted upon it even at grave personal cost. The great martyrs to virtue are named and universally honored. Gandhi, Bonhoeffer, and King, come quickly and easily to mind. Behind these exemplary giants are many lesser known but noble men and women, who, when it was their turn to lead, leaned against the prevailing culture winds of what was legal and made unpopular decisions simply because it was the good and right thing to do.

The Right Reverend William Henry Marmion was one of these honorable people. Even though "a son of the South," Marmion's Christian principles and beliefs called him to push against the prevailing culture of racism and Jim Crow. It would be the lay leadership of Christ Church that would strongly and publicly set in motion a multi-year struggle with their bishop over race. The confrontation would become increasingly ugly: some churchmen would refuse to give their bishop the courtesy of a handshake, and little of the usual funding was offered to Marmion to offset his expenses for attending the Lambeth Conference, the decadal meeting of bishops of the Anglican Communion world-wide.[88] Despite adversity, both personal and professional, Marmion's vision for the future of his diocese in southwest Virginia never wavered.

William Henry Marmion was born in Houston, Texas, on October 8, 1907.[89] Like many people of his generation, he spent his youth close to where he was born. He received his B.A. in 1929 from Rice University in Houston. The first time Marmion crossed the Mississippi River was when he was headed for Alexandria and the Virginia Theological Seminary with the $100 gifted to him by his Episcopal parish in his pocket.[90] Then as now, Episcopal seminary training was a combination of intense academic study and practical ministry. When the spring semester concluded, many seminarians went to hospitals

The Rt. Rev. William H. Marmion

in a big city to learn their chaplaining skills. Marmion took a different route and spent his summer ministering in one of the hardscrabble coal mining camps for the Erskine Coal Company in West Virginia. After the three years of requisite seminary education, Marmion graduated from Virginia Theological Seminary in 1932 with a Bachelor of Divinity degree.[91] All who knew him would attest that Marmion was thoughtful, careful, intentional, and studied. He was a remarkable, some might say obsessive, record keeper. He wrote in his journals about the theatrical and cinematic shows he saw, the books he read, his golf, and tennis scores. He was athletic, competitive, and mostly free of self-doubt. In his life, he would experience two World Wars, and, like many of his generation, he was philosophically more interested in the issues of peace and conflict than with the issues of racial justice that would be the hallmark of his later ministry. After his ordination to the priesthood in 1933, Marmion served for two years at two small Texas churches just outside of the state capital of Austin, St. James in Taylor and, twenty miles to the west, Grace Church in Georgetown.[92] In December of 1935, Marmion married Mabel Dougherty Hall; the two remained married for 66 years and had two children. Marmion left the Austin area for a call in San Antonio where he served for three years as the associate minister of St. Mark's Episcopal Church, a church that claimed Robert E. Lee as a member when Lee was a US Army lieutenant colonel in temporary command of the Department of Texas.[93] From San Antonio, Marmion accepted a call to St. Mary's Church-on-the-Highlands in Birmingham, Alabama. This must have been a good fit for both Marmion and St. Mary's, for Marmion remained rector for twelve years. In 1950, Marmion accepted the call to become rector of St. Andrew's Church in Wilmington, Delaware. St. Andrew's church would be Marmion's last cure as a parish priest.

The second Bishop of the Diocese of Southwestern Virginia, The Rt. Rev. Henry D. Phillips, was approaching his seventy-second birthday and described himself as being in ill health when, in 1953, he called for the election of his successor.[94] A search committee was formed in the diocese to evaluate and select nominees; Fred Woodson from Christ Church, Martinsville, was among those tapped for this important assignment. The search committee submitted a crowded field to the diocese; Marmion was one of the eight candidates chosen to stand for election at the Special Council.

With so many choices it was predicted that numerous ballots would be required to elect a bishop. With the notification to gather at St. John's Church in Roanoke for the Special Council, the delegates were warned to make overnight accommodations just in case the elections went long. As is the custom for the election of a bishop in the Episcopal Church, the lay delegates and the clergy delegates received their ballots separately and those ballots would be tallied separately. The successful candidate needed a majority of both the lay house and the clerical house. The leading candidate coming into the election was a "favorite son" from the Diocese of Southwestern Virginia, the Rev. Robert Magill of Lynchburg. Magill, as expected, jumped to an early lead in both houses on the first ballot.[95] On the second ballot Marmion received one more clergy vote than Magill but Magill collected more than twice as many lay votes as Marmion. By the third ballot Magill and Marmion were tied with the clergy votes, while Marmion made a substantial cut into Magill's lead in lay votes; all of the other candidates were in single digits in the voting in one or both houses. By the fourth ballot Marmion had achieved the needed clergy majority, but in the lay house Marmion was still two votes behind Magill and five votes from a majority. William Henry Marmion was elected the third Bishop of Southwestern Virginia on the fifth ballot by a slim margin of three votes above the majority in the clergy house and three votes above the majority in the lay house. To everyone's surprise, it was only 4:30 p.m. of the first day when the balloting ended.

After the election, and prior to his consecration as Bishop of Southwest Virginia, there was a highly unusual development in the Marmion family and the Episcopal Church: William Marmion attended the consecration of his older brother, Gresham, as Bishop of Kentucky. The Episcopal Church records the apostolic succession of its bishops back to the consecration of its first bishop, Samuel Seabury, in Scotland, on November 14, 1784. Each bishop is numbered in the order of succession, beginning with Seabury receiving the number 1. Gresham Marmion would claim number 527 in order of succession and William Marmion, 528. An uncommon occurrence for the church and the Marmion brothers, to say the least.

On May 13, 1954, William H. Marmion was consecrated bishop by the presiding bishop of the Episcopal Church, the Most Reverend Henry Knox Sherrill, along with the retiring Bishop Phillips of the diocese of Southwestern Virginia, and the recently consecrated Bishop of Kentucky, Gresham Marmion, the required minimum of three bishops needed for a valid sacrament. Eighteen other bishops of the church participated in this sacramental laying on of hands.[96] The rector of Christ Church, the Rev. Charles Fishburne, had a role in his bishop's consecration, serving as an assistant master of ceremonies. Not surprisingly, the lay members of Christ Church were well represented.[97]

The preacher for the service was seventy-year-old Bishop Clinton Simon Quin of Texas.[98] Quin was repeating a duty he had performed earlier in the Diocese of Kentucky for Gresham Marmion. Brothers Gresham and William Marmion credited Bishop Quin's influence on their decision to enter the ministry, and Quin accepted the invitation to preach at both of their consecrations. In true western style, the bishop of Texas arrived at the church wearing his cowboy hat. Following the service, there was a luncheon and reception for the new bishop, where Bishop Quin led the attendees in a rousing rendition of "The Eyes of Texas are Upon You." Marmion's former diocese, the Diocese of Delaware, presented the new bishop with the gift of a new black Buick automobile. The forty-six-year-old Marmion was ready and able to begin his new ministry in southwestern Virginia, with the full and joyous support of his people.

Marmion was bishop only three days when an event took place in Washington, DC, that would have thunderous repercussions for his ministry. The United States Supreme Court, in its unanimous decision in *Brown v. the Board of Education of Topeka,* ruled that the laws establishing "separate but equal" classrooms in public schools based on race were unconstitutional and ordered the racial integration of schools. This victory for racial equality would herald a new level of racial strife in the country and in the church. As he settled into his role as head of the diocese of Southwestern Virginia, all was quiet and cordial. But in very short order, Bishop Marmion would face the demanding and often thankless task of preparing his people to recognize the moral imperative of the times: striving for justice and peace among all people, and respecting the dignity of every human being.

11

Cardinal Parish, Cardinal Rector

Under the Rev. Philip Gresham, Christ Church in the mid-1950s was in its ascendancy in Martinsville and in the diocese of Southwestern Virginia. Christ Church was filled with active, powerful, influential men and women that the diocese looked to for leadership and support. That support included a heavy reliance by the diocese on Christ Church's financial contribution. When the diocese restructured its parish assessment program, Christ Church was one of four churches asked to continue their "generous giving" at the older higher rate during a "period of adjustment" for the diocese.[99] Coach Gresham's wrestlers may have tasted defeat on the mats of Climax High School gym, but Father Gresham's church was the epitome of a church holding sway. He was breathing the rarefied air of being at the top, and he was about to find out what a headache that can cause.

The first problem to be solved was one that every pastor of a congregation would love to tackle: Gresham's flock was literally bursting out of its doors. The vestry's response was to appoint R. M. Simmons Jr. to head up a planning committee to formulate recommendations for the future of the church.[100] The planning committee, in turn, felt it necessary to hire a consultant, Dr. Harry Atkinson, editor of the *Protestant Church Magazine*. In March of 1957, Christ Church's assistant superintendent for church school M. K. Jacobs, wrote to Atkinson detailing the scope of the space problem for the Sunday school. The detailed report included the number of classes, the registration for each and the location where the classes were held. The numbers were impressive: 14 classes for 174 children and teenagers, nursery age through high school. The two nurseries and two kindergarten classes accounted for 35 percent of the total. The issue for the vestry was space for all of these children. Five classes were in the church building. The other nine were in the rectory: first floor, second floor, living room, and basement. Even Christ Church's unmarried priest must have found this a difficult living arrangement.

After reading the church's report, Atkinson decided to go to Martinsville to survey the church facilities for himself. His analysis was a surprise to no one at Christ Church. "It is very evident from our study," he wrote, "that the educational facilities are very inadequate for present day procedures and needs. We found classes tucked away in cramped rooms where there was scarcely room for them to sit about tables.... We noted the lack of an adequate sacristy and offices for the administration work of the parish."

While acknowledging their current inadequacies, it was the hope of the committee that Atkinson could find a way so that the "present structure could be modified to accommodate 300 in the nave" and that room could be found for Sunday school classes with an anticipated average attendance of 250.[101] The consultant did not let the committee down easily: "I must frankly say that I seriously doubt the wisdom of trying to pack all the building space you need on your restricted site. This would be to your disadvantage and would make the rectory a rather unpleasant place for your clergyman especially if he has a family of growing children." At this point one could imagine the bachelor rector vigorously nodding in agreement with the expert's report. The issues laid out in his report made Atkinson's conclusion inescapable. The planning committee's consultant told them plainly that their "restricted site prohibits any appreciable growth or expansion of your buildings and programs." The vestry was told to buy more land.

At the point where the vestry heard the report and recommendations of the planning committee, they were also advised "that the report and recommendations be treated as 'confidential.'"[102] One of the first issues the committee struggled with was the optimal size of a congregation. They referred the vestry to a recent piece in the respected Episcopal magazine, *The Living Church,* entitled, "Bigger or Better?" The article stated that after interviewing priests and bishops about the problem of parochial size, "all of them state that a parish, which exceeds 500 communicants has moved across the line, which separates a family from a mob." Gresham heartily agreed with this analysis. He felt that if a parish were to grow much larger than 500 communicants, "the priest has difficulty in meeting his responsibilities in the parish and maintaining a close relationship with the members of his church."

The committee reported they spent considerable time agonizing over the prospect of leaving downtown Martinsville and reestablishing the church further out from the center of the city. While such a move would allow for the physical expansion of the church, it would move Christ Church from what was currently the center of the parish map and lead to the view that it was becoming a neighborhood church. Rejecting the idea of a move, the committee considered new construction on the existing property. However, they repeated their consultant's warning that any expansion would run the risk of overcrowding the current lot. The obvious solution was to purchase property beside or behind the church. To this end, committee members spoke to the neighbors about their willingness sell. The closest they came was hearsay that the neighboring Pannill mansion, currently owned by seven family members, would probably go on the real estate market upon the death of the family matriarch, who was the sole family member living there. However, this was a topic that no one in the family wished to discuss until that eventuality. With their analysis of the problem exhausted, the committee made its recommendation to the vestry: "To lay it right on the line, we feel that the future of Christ Church should be tied in with the property across the street." The property recommended to the vestry for purchase was owned by the Smith family.

The vestry commended the committee for its "splendid study and report" and appointed a small, select committee of vestrymen, Charles C. Broun and Thomas J. Burch, to "attempt to negotiate for the purchase of the Smith property." By December of 1958, the special committee returned to the vestry with a proposal for a "rental-purchase option arrangement" where the church would rent the Smith property for three to five years at a rent not to exceed $125.00 a month and an option to purchase it for a price not to exceed $47,000.[103] In February 1959, the vestry heard that they had a deal for the Smith property, 316 East Church Street, across the street from the church. It was agreed that Junior Warden Clarence P. Kearfott, who was also an attorney, be instructed to prepare an agreement effective April 1, 1959. During the first week of March 1959, while Kearfott worked on preparing papers for the lease/purchase of the Smith house, the vestry learned that the Pannill mansion, the very desirable property next to the church at the crest of Scuffle Hill, was available for purchase.

The house on Scuffle Hill was the answer to a prayer for the Christ Church vestry. Adjacent to and just west of Christ Church's property, it provided the ideal site for the expansion of the church's campus. By comparison, the Smith house, located across Church Street, would force children going to and from Sunday school to negotiate one of Martinsville's major roadways. The Pannill Mansion was literally right next door, on the pinnacle of Scuffle Hill, so named by William Letcher Pannill, who acquired the property in the midst of the Great Depression and joked about his purchase "because it was located on a hill and he had to scuffle to pay for it."[104] The membership was willing to accept a silly name for their campus location in exchange for sole ownership of the view from the top.

The walls of the two-story Pannill mansion were all that remained of the first distinguished home to occupy the site. In 1904, the 10.58 acres at 311 East Church Street was deeded to the former president of Liggett and Myers Tobacco Company, Benjamin F. Stevens. It was he who built the three-story mansion known as Oak Hall that dominated the landscape of turn-of-the-century Martinsville. The magnificence of the house he built caused not a few visitors in town to mistake it for the Henry County courthouse; strangers to town would picnic on the front lawn, thinking they were eating on the grass of the public square.[105] The attraction to the house was undeniable. The claim was that from the top floor on a clear day, one could see as far as Moore's Knob in North Carolina, 50 miles away, as well as the "inspiring heights of the Blue Ridge in Franklin and Patrick counties." It might also be true, as was claimed in 1917, that the fire that started in the basement and gutted the house glowed as far.

At the time of the fire, the house was occupied by Stevens' daughter and her husband Pannill Rucker. The family had insured the house for $20,000 and its contents for $10,000, a goodly sum for 1917, but not near enough for a home of such elegance that contained one of the finest collections of arts and antiques in Virginia.[106] The damage to the house and its contents was estimated to be in excess of $125,000. Still, the fire did not result in a total loss. Using the four walls left standing, Rucker began to rebuild the house, but this time with only two stories instead of three. In 1920 Pannill Rucker moved to Richmond and the house, yet unfinished, was sold to Rives S. Brown, who completed construction and lived in the building until 1933. It was that year that William Pannill moved into the mansion with his wife and children, six daughters and one son, renaming the property Scuffle Hill. Pannill's children grew up and moved out of the mansion, and the death of William Pannill in 1940, left only his widow in the massive house.

Although reduced from its original three to just two stories, the Pannill House was still commandingly large. Centered on the porch and framed with four massive columns, the front door opened into a spacious foyer, dominated by a magnificent staircase with polished wood bannisters. On the east and west of the second-floor hall were two sets of bedrooms with connecting bathrooms that could easily be converted to four Sunday school classrooms. Additional rooms on the second floor could be used for office space or meetings. The main floor had a formal dining room, paneled library, music room, sitting room, kitchen, and a sunroom in the rear of the building; all of the main rooms on both floors contained a fireplace. Besides the living areas the house had thousands of square feet of attic and basement space. For Christ Church's space problem, the house on Scuffle Hill seemed heaven sent.

At the March 4 meeting of the vestry, it was decided that a "quiet but expert appraisal" be made of the Pannill property. This discreet assessment did not put a stop to the vestry's plans for acquiring the Smith property; on April 1, Christ Church concluded a purchase-rental agreement for 316 East Church Street. With the Sunday school year about to end, Gresham and the church's Sunday school superintendent began plans for immediate use of the Smith property. However, by May, the Pannill family had agreed to sell the house on Scuffle Hill to the church for $100,000 with a one-third down payment.[107] The vestry was in a buying mood and unanimously voted to authorize a committee consisting of R. M. Simmons Sr., R. M. Simmons Jr., Charles C. Broun, Stafford G. Whittle III, and Clarence P. Kearfott to find the "ways and means of financing the cost of acquisition." Christ Church would have all the space it needed, and then some!

The Rev. Philip M. Gresham could justifiably believe that he had reached a milestone in his vocation as a priest in the month of May in 1959. A year previous, his congregation was overflowing the church's property on Sunday morning, from reredos to rectory. A month previous, his congregation had acquired the property across the street on a lease-purchase agreement, and with the ink hardly dry on that contract, the family that owned the church's dream property proffered a deal for the house next door. Then, just because things needed to be even more complicatedly wonderful, R. S. Brown Jr. "indicated his willingness and desire to deed (without cost) to Christ Church a tract of land owned by Mr. Brown and his firm, Lanier Farm, Inc. and located off the recently-developed extension of Corn Tassel Trail, as a site for a second Episcopal Church in Martinsville."[108] Who would believe it! The vestry accepted this "gracious offer" but failed to state for the minutes that there already was a "second" Episcopal Church in Martinsville," the African-American St. Paul's Episcopal Church. By June, the special committee had put together a plan for a four-year capital campaign to pay for the Pannill property plus an additional $25,000 for improvements including parking. The sum of

$30,000 was made as down payment, and possession of Scuffle Hill by the church was scheduled for July 1. Incredibly, nothing was ever heard again of the tract of land on Corn Tassel Trail nor was the idea of a third church in Martinsville ever revisited by the vestry.

On Sunday, September 13, 1959, a procession led by a crucifer, flag bearers, and the youth Canterbury choir made its way from the church to Christ Church's parish house, Oak Hall's newest name. Standing with Junior Warden Kearfott and the superintendent of the Sunday school, B. S. Parrish, Gresham blessed and dedicated the congregation's new acquisition for the upbuilding of the church. Future Junior Warden Trippi Penn, dressed in his junior choir robe, was photographed for the *Martinsville Bulletin*'s coverage of this event. On the day they took possession of Scuffle Hill, there was no denying the incredible success of Christ Episcopal Church and its rector.

It is one of the recurring struggles of Christianity not to let evangelistic success drown out the good news it proclaims. It took only 300 years for Christianity, from the morning when its entire membership could gather in one place in a house on Pentecost, to grow into the state religion of the Roman Empire. Christianity has struggled with the benefits and consequences of success ever since. By the grace of God, the Rev. Philip Gresham in his very first call as leader of a congregation found himself in a cardinal parish. With youthful energy and hard work, Christ Church's rector, only thirty years old, had become one of the Diocese of Southwestern Virginia's success stories. As a rising star in one of the diocese's preeminent churches, most everyone agreed Gresham had earned the right to the mantle of a cardinal rector with all of the power and authority that goes with it. But would it be enough for the challenges he faced now and the ones that lay ahead?

12

"Some Mighty Fine Christians..."

Acquiring a building, even with the debt it entails, is a leadership burden easily embraced since it is the gratifying affliction of growth and success; it is the joyous stress of the abundant harvest. However, while rector and vestry pulled together to achieve Scuffle Hill, at the same time, there lurked a different leadership trial for them of a most punishing nature: a test of moral leadership. The canons of the Episcopal Church, the rules for the governance of the church, give the rector in charge of a congregation an enormous amount of authority for leading the congregation, but authority is not the same as power. Power is wedded to authority when the congregation accepts the rector's proven leadership. Only when the rector uses moral authority to move a congregation in a positive direction, often a direction the people are reluctant to go, does a rector become a true pastoral leader. This exercise of pastoral power and authority is predictably difficult and dangerous to the priest's standing with his or her people. Only when the rector is willing to risk disappointing the congregation at a level they can tolerate does leadership happen.[109] In the late 1950s, in the Diocese of Southwestern Virginia, there were ample opportunities to disappoint a congregation, and nowhere was this more true than at Christ Episcopal Church in Martinsville. Even as they enthusiastically negotiated the expansion of the Christ Church campus the vestry bristled when word was leaked that the Executive Board of the diocese had divided over Bishop Marmion's plan to present to the 1958 Diocesan Council his proposal for the racial integration of the Hemlock Haven Camp & Conference Center.

As early as 1955, Bishop Marmion had established the policy for racial inclusion in his diocese. The year after his consecration as bishop, Marmion announced that a policy for full participation at diocesan meetings would mean there would be no distinction because of race or color. Despite the bishop's very public statement of this policy at his first annual Diocesan Council, the Christ Church vestry reacted with indignant surprise when it was reported at the regular March vestry meeting that Hemlock Haven would be integrated. The vestry minutes of March 4, 1958, registered their shock:

> In discussing the summer conferences to be held at Hemlock Haven—property recently purchased by the diocese to be used as a permanent conference center—The vestry learned that as a matter of diocesan policy the center will be available to all communicants of the diocese, regardless of race or color. Members of the vestry not only took issue with this policy—of integration—but also indicated their desire that the vestry take some official action in opposition to the policy. The vestry agreed to discuss this matter further at a special meeting to be held March 18, 1958, at 7:30 p.m. in the Ruth Redd Room.[110]

For the first time the Rev. Philip Gresham faced one of the major burdens of his vocation, the realization that being a solo rector can be a lonely calling. Only eighteen months prior to this meeting, Gresham had the security of being a curate in a large Richmond church with an older, wiser priest to turn to for help in a crisis. In Martinsville, he was priest-in-charge and pretty much on his own.

That night of March 4, after presiding over what must have been a long, arduous vestry meeting, Gresham returned to his empty rectory. Unable to sleep, the weary rector of Christ Church sat at his typewriter to compose a letter to his bishop:

> My dear Bishop,
>
> At the regular monthly meeting of the Vestry this evening, I informed my men of the policy in effect at the new conference center regarding integration. Since I talked to Bill Reardon last week, this was thought to be the best time for such news. I did want to sit down and write to you about that meeting, knowing what concern you must have about reactions in the diocese.
>
> Naturally, such news has hurt most of my men a great deal. Their first reaction was one of anger and hostility. It wasn't a loud wounded kind of hostility; but somewhat subdued. Naturally, some were more talkative than others. I'm afraid the few who support this decision did not speak at all.
>
> Much concern has been felt over the fact that they weren't told sooner. They have been mighty proud of their giving to the Diocesan needs, especially at present, over which resentment has been shown tonight! There was slight intimation of "not doing so well next year." One member suggested that he might

not pledge to the parish as much next year, but other members of the vestry warned him not to say anything he would regret.

Our discussion lasted about an hour. I presented the Diocesan policy, with which I am in full accord.

Perhaps I should talk over this matter with you personally. But I've got to talk to somebody tonight. The vestry realized the explosive nature of such news, for the parish, and the city. We shall meet again in two weeks to discuss it further.

And please don't get the slightest idea that this was a knock-down-drag-out brawl. From the outset the deep love of these men for each other, and for their church, and for me, has been evident. It was a humbling experience. It has brought us all more...[at this point an entire line of Gresham's letter is lost because of a tear in the paper]...sition, not my own. We left that meeting, I do believe, with a deeper love for one another than before. The Holy Spirit was with us almost as thickly as was the cigarette smoke!

There will surely be yet more pain in this parish, Bishop. But, despite the initial anger, great wisdom in their thinking has come out. Some mighty fine Christians are segregationist. As feelings run now, the summer conferences will be greatly hurt. Some families will probably send their children into North Carolina for this kind of experience. Between now and when the Vestry meets again, hysteria might have taken over.

But I did want you to know the way things stand as of now.

Devotedly in Service,
Phil Gresham[111]

While this letter resides in the diocesan archives with other correspondence from Gresham to his bishop there is no record of any meeting or additional letters between Bishop Marmion and Philip Gresham in the two weeks between the March 4 and March 18 vestry meetings, though it is almost unimaginable that Marmion let Gresham's letter pass without a response. Certainly, Gresham knew that he needed to prepare for the upcoming vestry meeting. It is highly likely that he consulted with his bishop about the diocesan policy for the camp and conference center. It is just as likely that Bishop Marmion would offer guidance personally—as Gresham had suggested in his letter—for the proper approach to take with the Christ Church vestry about the sensitive issue of integration.

At 7:30 p.m. on March 18, Gresham began the special Christ Church vestry meeting with a prayer. Sitting around the table with their rector were Justice Kennon C. Whittle, senior warden; Clarence P. Kearfott, junior warden; treasurer Warren J. Watrous, secretary W. H. Yeaman, and fellow vestrymen Robert B. Mercer, Dr. F. Paul Turner Jr., H. Kenneth Whitener, John R. Whittle, John K. Adams, Charles C. Broun, Thomas J. Burch, T. F. Gilliam, Gordon W. Olson, Francis T. West, William C. Cole Jr., Julian F. Hirst, Donald R. Strachan, Charles D. Weaver, and Fred V. Woodson Jr. It was noted in the minutes that all members were present, with the lone exception of the Sunday school superintendent, B. S. Parrish.

We should not pass without noting that this was a gathering of Old Dominion gentry. One might suggest without fear of contradiction that any major corporation in Virginia would have been fortunate to have this group of men as their board of directors. Sitting with Gresham was a state supreme court justice, former and future Martinsville mayors, prominent attorneys, and influential business owners—all of them esteemed Episcopal churchmen who had served at the National

Convention and Diocesan Council, acted as choir director and organist, as licensed lay reader and Sunday school teacher, sat on bishop and rector call committees and, of course, on the vestry of a leading Episcopal Church. These members of the Virginia elite had gathered to make their influential voice heard on the topic of the racial integration of a church youth camp.

Generally, the agenda for a "special meeting" would be restricted to the topic for which the meeting was called. Perhaps, aware of the gravity of what they were about to do, the Christ Church Vestry chose to brace themselves for the task at hand by dealing with other, less controversial, issues first. They began with an interim report from the treasurer and approved the payment of the cost of a new surplice for the rector. Next, they unanimously appointed Clarence Kearfott and Paul Turner as delegates and Robert Mercer and Francis West as alternates to the Diocesan Council meeting May 15–17 in Roanoke.

With the preliminaries out of the way, Gresham reviewed with the vestry the "official" announcement of the summer youth conferences at Hemlock Haven. The vestry secretary recorded that Gresham went on to state the "official position of the church with respect to racial integration and/or segregation, referring to the General Convention Resolution of 1955, the Council Address of Bishop Marmion delivered in 1955 as well as his (the Rector's) own position—all endorsing and supporting racial integration—as the basis for the contemplated intermingling of the races at the forthcoming diocesan summer conferences."

Upon the conclusion of the review, Charles Broun moved and Francis West seconded the adoption of a lengthy resolution. Given the precision of the language, it is extremely unlikely that this resolution was not prepared ahead of time and reviewed by most if not all of the vestry members prior to the meeting. The resolution reads:

WHEREAS, at the last regular meeting of the Vestry of Christ Church, Martinsville, Virginia, we were informed for the first time that the Youth Conference of the Diocese would be held this summer at the Church camp near Hungry Mother Park, on an integrated basis, and

WHEREAS, the Vestry feels that such an integrated meeting of the youth of the Church is both illegal and ill-advised, and

WHEREAS, the history of the Episcopal Church in Virginia from its inception has been on a segregated basis, and

WHEREAS, the laws of this sovereign Commonwealth expressly forbid the intermingling of the races as contemplated by the Bishop of our Diocese in the holding of the Youth Conference as aforesaid, and

WHEREAS, we do not subscribe to the reasoning behind this new "judicial sin" and are unwilling to participate in the violation of the laws of the Commonwealth;

NOW, THEREFORE, BE IT RESOLVED, by the Vestry of Christ Episcopal Church of Martinsville, Virginia, in meeting assembled on this the 18th day of March, 1958:

First: That the Vestry heartily disapproves of the contemplated integrated youth meeting.

Second: We are confused regarding the rules governing the proposed conference, our understanding being that there will be no intimate association permitted between the children of the two races, which leaves us in a quandary as to where integration begins or where it ends, thus posing the question to be resolved by Christians: Where does the "sin" begin and where does it end?

Third: We definitely feel that we should have been told the "whole truth" when we were asked to contribute to the recreational center, and we hereby go on record as being opposed to further payments from our Church to the same.

Fourth: We further definitely request and in the future will demand full information regarding solicitation of funds going to the Diocese or the general Church, bearing on the efforts of either to nullify the intent and purpose here expressed.

Fifth: We feel the above is in keeping with Christian reasoning in that the intermingling of the races, in addition to being illegal, can, in our view, only lead to bitterness, discord, and confusion among our people, which will be a greater "sin" than that pronounced by judicial decree.

Sixth: We urge the Members of the Congregation to save their children embarrassment by keeping them from the proposed Conference.

BE IT FURTHER RESOLVED that a copy of this Resolution be mailed to the adult Members of the Congregation, and a copy be delivered to the Bishop of the Diocese, by a committee of the Vestry, and a copy mailed to the Chairman of the Department of Christian Education.

The resolution was "almost unanimously adopted (vestryman Clarence H. Burrage being recorded as "against"). The minutes do not record that there was any discussion of the resolution with the exception of the intriguing hint that the motion and second for adoption was for the "resolution, as amended." There is no way to determine from the minutes what was added or subtracted.

Knowing the positions taken by both their bishop and their rector, the vestry tried to soften the blow of what they had just done by concluding the meeting with the following statement for the minutes: "The Vestry, in adopting the resolution, expressed its cognizance of the Rector's position and feelings in the matter as well as its love and respect for him. The Vestry, too, indicated that in no way did it wish to discredit or jeopardize the effective leadership or accomplishments of either the Bishop of the diocese or the Rector."[112]

The influence of the Episcopal Church in Virginia and of Christ Episcopal Church in Martinsville in particular was on display when five days after the vestry met, the Sunday edition of the *Roanoke Times,* the major "big city" daily paper for many in Martinsville, ran a three-inch banner headline on page B-1, "MARTINSVILLE VESTRY PROTESTS PROPOSAL FOR MIXING RACES: Episcopalians Plan for integrated Camp in Smyth."[113] The article reported that Bishop Marmion "declined comment when asked about the Martinsville church's action." After several paragraphs of explanatory notes including misnaming the Senior Warden as Virginia Supreme Court Justice Vernon C. Whittle, the article ended by reprinting the Christ Church vestry's resolution in its entirety.

The *Martinsville Bulletin* picked up the story from the Associated Press and ran a banner headline, "CHRIST CHURCH VESTRY HERE OPPOSES INTEGRATED CAMP."[114] The *Bulletin*'s report drew heavily from quotes from an abbreviated version of the vestry's resolution. The next day things took a bizarre turn when competing stories appeared in Monday's newspapers that alleged that Gresham had resigned while other papers denied any resignation by Christ Church's rector. The *Roanoke Times* ran a picture of Gresham with the banner, "RESIGNATION SAID GIVEN BY MARTINSVILLE RECTOR."[115] The report stated that Gresham had resigned

Sunday morning but that the resignation could not be confirmed or denied. "An informed source told the *Times* Mr. Gresham turned in his resignation to church officials after the morning service." However, the *Times* went on to admit they could not contact Gresham to confirm his resignation. The article was peppered with quotes from the vestry's resolution and the speculation that the alleged resignation was linked to the vestry's action on integration. Later on Monday, more newspaper articles about the unconfirmed resignation appeared. In one account, AP was tagged as the source. A picture of Gresham ran next to the article; under his name was printed "...No Resignation." The headline for the article stated, "GRESHAM DENIES REPORT HE OFFERED RESIGNATION."[116] Quoting Gresham, the article reported, "I have not resigned and have no intention of resigning." The article went on to say that the AP had located Bishop Marmion in Baltimore for comment. The bishop's reply was that anything concerning the matter would have to come from either Gresham or the Christ Church vestry. As in previous articles, readers were given a summary version of the vestry resolution and Christ Church's opposition to racial integration. In a newspaper clipping taken from the Christ Church archives, dateline "Martinsville, March 24 (special)" the headline reads, "MARTINSVILLE RECTOR DENIES RESIGNATION."[117] This clipping, from an unknown newspaper, repeats what others had reported. The article states that Gresham told a reporter," I have not resigned and I have no intention of resigning." It goes on to rehash Christ Church's opposition to racial integration and Bishop Marmion's thoughts that whatever was going on with Gresham's resignation, "...is a matter for the Martinsville church to decide." The only bit of information about Gresham's mood in these chaotic days comes at the conclusion of this article: "Efforts to reach the Rev. Mr. Gresham Sunday afternoon and night and early today to confirm the report that he had announced his resignation failed. He said this afternoon that he had 'retreated into seclusion.'"

It is unknown if or where Gresham found the seclusion he desired. The news of his church's stand on racial integration was on the news wires and being republished around the country. The *Florence Times* in Florence, Alabama, ran a news story about the Martinsville church, "INTEGRATED YOUTH CONFERENCE CAUSES RIFT IN CHURCH."[118]

What became the accepted version of what happened following the March 18 meeting—according to a later *Bulletin* report—is that Gresham asked Marmion to relieve him of his duties as rector of Christ Church and the bishop refused.[119] For the time being, Gresham and the vestry would have to work to find a way to live with their differences.

13

A Diocese in Turmoil

On April 17, 1958, the Executive Board of the diocese summoned the head of the Department of Christian Education for the diocese, the Rev. Dr. Richard Beasley, to report on "the so-called policy of integration for Hemlock Haven."[120] Chaired by the bishop and comprised of clergy and lay members, the executive board was the business arm of the diocese, comparable to the vestry of a church. The May Diocesan Council meeting was approaching, and the board wanted more information before they could make recommendations on the 1959 budget for Hemlock Haven. Beasley began by reminding the board that the decision to hold a racially integrated youth camp "was not set up overnight" nor was it superimposed "from the top." Beasley went over a brief history of the church's movement in the direction of full integration of the races, beginning with the General Convention's resolution in 1952 calling on the church to help relieve racial discrimination in our country. He reminded the board that in 1956, Bishop Marmion published a letter in the diocesan newsletter, "The *Southwestern Episcopalian,*" stating that "at such time as the diocese would have a conference center, it would provide us with a place which could be used by all of our people." The racial integration of Hemlock Haven "had not come out of thin-air" and it had "a definite background." When Beasley finished, the chancellor of the diocese, C. Francis Cocke, spoke to the matter. He informed the executive board that he and the bishop had had a lengthy and frank discussion about the integration of Hemlock Haven, a position that Cocke did not support. At the end of their discussion, Cocke, the man who had been the legal counselor for the diocese since its organization in 1919,[121] said he had offered the bishop his resignation as diocesan chancellor. Despite their differences, the bishop asked that Cocke not resign. The chancellor returned to the matter at hand. Relying on his considerable understanding of both church canon law and the polity of the Episcopal church, Cocke raised with the board "the question of whether or not the bishop, by pronouncement, could adopt a policy which so plainly affects the laity of the diocese." Turning next to civil law, Cocke went on to explain that "the policy of the State has been clearly stated by the legislative action; that the diocesan policy now finds itself in the position of moving squarely into the face of the law of the Commonwealth." The diocesan chancellor concluded his remarks with the ominous warning "that a real and deep sorrow is being experienced throughout the diocese over this matter, and that a financial reaction is bound to be reflected in next year's diocesan efforts."

The lay members of the executive board leapt up to agree with Chancellor Cocke. Yuille Holt spoke of the deep distress of many of the church people of Lynchburg "over the turn of events" and suggested "that if both races are to use Hemlock Haven, it would be better to have separate conferences and camp groups." Walter Stephenson of Roanoke was quick to agree, stating that he was "definitely not in sympathy with an integrated camp program" and that his conversations with other Episcopalians reinforced the chancellor's prediction that the policy of integration of the camp and conference programs "will lead to serious curtailment in our financial efforts."

The clergy of the executive board, for their part, stood with their bishop. The Rev. Henry Fox reminded his colleagues that in the bishop's 1955 diocesan council address, Marmion had stated that the diocese needed "a place of our own where all our people can come without being discriminated against."

A motion was made and seconded that Hemlock Haven be opened on a non-integrated basis, but in a vote of 11 to 5, the motion was tabled. The executive board had reached an impasse. The matter of Hemlock Haven would be taken up by the entire diocesan council meeting in Roanoke in May.

By the time the diocesan council met in Roanoke in May of 1958, Bishop Marmion had received letters from eleven of the sixty-six vestries in the diocese voicing opposition to the planned integration of the summer programs at Hemlock Haven.[122] The diocesan chancellor continued his opposition to his bishop, insisting that there was an attempt to sneak integration past the lay people of the diocese. "Laymen of the diocese," Cocke said, "were 'kept in ignorance of it until newspaper accounts revealed it in reports of protests of the vestry of Christ Church, Martinsville.'"[123]

The diocesan council of 1958 in Roanoke would be remembered as a legislative contest between the clergy and the lay members. The meeting was notable for the parliamentary maneuvering by groups of delegates with repeated breaks in the meeting so that the clergy and the lay members could caucus separately. The maneuver of choice for the lay delegates depended on Article Six of the constitution of the Diocese of Southwestern Virginia, which stated that "in all matters before the Council, the clergy and the laity shall deliberate in one body and a majority shall give validity to any measure, but when five members request it there shall be a vote by orders and a majority of each order shall be necessary to a decision." Where Hemlock Haven was concerned, most of the actions were voted on by orders.

The first motion on Hemlock Haven was on a "compromise resolution" drawn up by the deadlocked executive board that called for no youth conferences for the summer of 1958 and for a committee appointed by the executive board to study integration proposals for a year.[124] Immediately a substitute motion was proposed by a group that the *Roanoke World News* described as a "rump conference of leading laymen" that had met "late into the night." Their proposal held that "youth conferences shall be held during the coming summer in keeping with the customs heretofore observed, and appropriate arrangements be made for separate conferences during the coming summer for Colored youth of the diocese."[125] In making the substitute motion on the floor of the Council, Baldwin Locher, a delegate from Glasgow who served in the Virginia legislature, stated that it was offered "'with no desire to cause controversy but with the feeling that it is unfair to deprive children of the use of Hemlock Haven because of a difference of opinion regarding its operation."[126] The discussion on the two motions continued until council business was paused for noonday prayer, followed by lunch.

When the council returned to business, the delegates were presented with a substitute to Locher's substitute motion to solve the problem of the youth summer program.[127] The Rev. John H. Teeter from Trinity Church Rocky Mount proposed "that youth conferences at Hemlock Haven be operated this summer on the basis of racial integration and sexual segregation" with a biracial commission appointed to study the problem. Council delegate and Commonwealth legislator Robert Whitehead called for a vote by orders and was supported by the required number of delegates. Teeter's substitute measure was defeated in the lay order, with the laity voting 21 for it and 64 against, while the clergy agreed with Teeter, voting 34 for the proposal and 10 against. This early compromise for integration by race but segregation by gender could be characterized as the "Perennial Resolution" for the number of times it rose up only to die and rise again whenever Hemlock Haven was debated.

Following the defeat of Teeter's proposal, a vote was called for Locher's substitute motion for racially separated camps. This time, the resolution was defeated in the clerical order with only 5 clergy voting for the measure and 39 against it, while the lay delegates voted 65 in favor and 17 against. With both of the substitute motions defeated, the call was made to vote on the original motion put forward by the executive board to cancel youth camp for the summer of 1958. The measure was defeated in the lay order, with 54 of the 80 voting lay members voting against closing the camp, while only 9 of the 44 voting clergy agreed with them.

On an early May evening, it is doubtful that the diocesan council in Roanoke was on the minds of many Episcopalians in Martinsville or in any of the towns and villages of southwestern Virginia. After a week of work or school, it was time to enjoy a warm spring weekend and begin to make plans for the summer. While preparing to relax with the evening paper of Friday, May 16, Christ Church members were confronted with a front-page story in the late edition of the *Roanoke World News,* carrying the headline, "EPISCOPAL DIOCESE SHARPLY SPLIT ON INTEGRATION ISSUE."[128] The youth camp controversy that began in the Christ Church vestry room was threatening to divide the diocese.

In his Council Message on Friday evening in Roanoke, Bishop Marmion reminded his diocese that the "main purpose" of a diocesan-owned conference center was the hope that "we would not have to say 'No' as we have been compelled to do in the past to our Negro Young people who have applied."[129] Marmion went on to state that the design for integration proposed for the diocese was modeled on the successful policies of the nearby dioceses in Delaware, Maryland, the District of Columbia, West Virginia, and Kentucky. In most of those dioceses the "pressure of numbers" was much larger than in the diocese of Southwestern Virginia, he said, "where only five out of 66 congregations are non-white" and "only approximately 125 of the 9,700 communicants are Negro." Addressing the issue of whether the church would be in violation of the Commonwealth's laws for racial segregation of public assemblies the bishop pointed out that "Hemlock Haven is private property owned by the Diocese of Southwestern Virginia. Our conferences are not open to the public."[130] The bishop acknowledged that there "are honest differences of opinion in regard to the manner, speed and extent of applying" the process of racial integration to the church's youth conferences.[131] However, Marmion would not excuse differences in response to Christian discipleship. "God's commandments are binding on everyone," he said. "His judgment rests on all of our arrangements short of his will. We must move in the direction which seems to the church to be his will."[132] The bishop had given his people much to ponder as they made their way to their homes and hotel rooms that night.

Saturday morning greeted a deeply divided Diocesan Council. No sooner did the bishop call the session to order than a motion was made to grant a recess so that the clerical and lay delegates could caucus separately. And caucus they did, the entire morning session. After noonday prayer both the lay and the clerical delegates put forth separate resolutions on Hemlock Haven, but before they could get started with debate, a request was made to postpone discussion so that other diocesan business could be dealt with. It was not until late in the afternoon that Robert Whitehead rose to move the lay delegates' resolution; it stated:

> 1) The Conference Center at Hemlock Haven be operated until Council shall decide otherwise, on the following basis: (a) All exclusively adult conferences shall be open on an unrestricted basis, as has been the practice in the past. (b) All youth and children conferences, each of which is now scheduled to be twelve days duration, shall be divided into two periods of equal time length, the first to be restricted to white youth and children, the second to be unrestricted. 2) This Council shall elect and appoint a study commission of nineteen members, ten white laymen to be elected by the lay delegates in caucus assembled, four clergy to be elected by the clerical members in caucus assembled, three laywomen to be elected by the women's auxiliary, and two Negro members to be appointed by the bishop. Any vacancies on this Commission shall be filled by the Commission itself, the same numerical proportions to be maintained. The Commission shall elect its own officers. It shall be the duty of this Commission to study the whole problem, to visit all areas of the diocese and discuss the problem with communicants of the church, and to report to the Executive Board by February 1, 1959. The Executive Board shall advise the bishop whether a special meeting of Council shall be called. A report shall be made to the May 1959 meeting of Council.[133]

In the discussion that followed, this resolution came to be known as the "double track" plan with a six-day session open to whites only, and a six-day session open to anyone.[134] In a vote by orders, the resolution was doomed. As expected the "double track" plan had the overwhelming support of the lay caucus; 59 of 70 lay delegates voted in favor. However, by a margin of 2 to 1 the clergy rejected the plan: 12 clergy voted for the measure while twice as many, 24, opposed it. Delegate Robert Whitehead was furious at the outcome of the vote. "We have reached the point of no return," he declared.[135] The clergy were equally adamant about their position. They saw a vote for the "double track" plan as "giving aid and support to segregationists." One priest described the attitude among the clergy as "unwilling to take part in any 'Jim Crow' young people's conference." Another priest said that the plan was "morally ambiguous; it evaded the issue and passed the buck to our children."

With the lay motion gone down in flames, the clergy presented their plan. The clergy deleted from the lay proposal the "double track" plan but offered, with the exact same wording used in the second part of the Lay resolution, a call for a study commission. This motion carried in both orders with the clergy unanimously in favor and the laity narrowly consenting, voting 36 in favor while 31 opposed. Among the laymen elected by the convention to the study commission was Christ Church Martinsville vestryman and ardent segregationist, Francis T. West. With a study commission charged to recommend a solution to the youth camp issue, the diocesan council in the last of its sessions voted as one body to shut down the youth program for 1958. By a vote of 67 for and 32 against, the Council accepted the following motion: "Resolved that there be no youth conference at Hemlock Haven this summer."[136]

Among the other notable actions of the 1958 diocesan council was the defeat for the second year in a row of a change to the diocesan canons to allow women to serve on vestries. The clergy voted 21 in favor and 9 opposed while only 5 lay delegates voted in favor and 39 voted against women on vestries.[137] Voting by congregation is nowhere recorded; however, it is a safe assumption that the Martinsville delegation from Christ Church heeded their vestry's instruction from the previous year to vote against allowing women on vestries.[138]

There was no denying that the 39th Annual Council of the Diocese of Southwestern Virginia ended with some very bruised feelings on the part of its delegates. A few of the clergy felt that a decision to integrate the diocesan conference center was a question of church doctrine and wholly the prerogative of the bishop. According to the *Roanoke Times*, these priests believed that "only temporal matters of the church are within the policymaking scope of the general Council" and integration was seen as a moral and spiritual matter.[139] The long-serving chancellor of the diocese argued that moving from the historic segregation of the church was a matter of policy and only the general council could change policy. After seeing his proposal go down to defeat, the *Roanoke Times* reported, Baldwin Locher "took to the floor to criticize the clergy's conduct in the controversy. He argued that the clergy have some obligation to laymen other than 'pushing us around.'" For his part, Robert Whitehead warned that by forcing the issue, the clergy bore the responsibility for the canceled youth conferences at Hemlock Haven and might be guilty as well of discouraging future contributions to diocesan funds. Speaking of his fellow lay delegates, Whitehead declared, "We have done everything we could to meet the ends of justice."[140]

14

"The Unfortunate Controversy Which Has Arisen"

Meeting on May 14, in advance of the 1958 diocesan council in Roanoke, the vestry of Christ Church had decided to take "no action" after receiving a report that the Executive Board of the diocese had adopted and would propose at Council a resolution "stating that youth conferences will not be conducted at the diocesan conference center (Hemlock Haven) this year." After days of contentious sessions, the Council's final action was in line with the Executive Board's proposal. Satisfied, the vestry whose letter opposing the integration of Hemlock Haven had thrown the diocese into turmoil, returned to business as usual. When the Christ Church vestry gathered for its June meeting, the treasurer asked about "the 1958 pledges to the diocese, which the vestry indicated it might withhold for reasons set forth in its resolution of March 18, 1958."[141] Since the diocesan council had blocked Bishop Marmion's attempts at racial integration in the diocese, it seems vestry members felt they could be generous in victory; they "instructed the treasurer to honor the pledges as funds become available." The vestry then adjourned for the summer.

In Martinsville, everything slowed down for the summer. Martinsville High School would graduate its senior class, and the new graduates would celebrate with a picnic at Fairy Stone State Park fifteen miles out of town and up the mountains. The Martinsville High School yearbook handed out at the end of the year contained the usual half page ad generously contributed by Christ Church. In 1958, the separation of church and state was unapologetically ignored in Virginia. Christian clubs were popular with the students and well supported by the school administration and faculty. One exception to the school's promotion of this breach in the wall of separation was the school's wrestling coach, the Rev. Phil Gresham.[142] Gresham's scholarly Anglican tradition permitted little tolerance for the Biblical fundamentalism of the boy's HiY or the girl's Omega Tri-HiY Christian organizations at the high school. Like a good shepherd, he guarded his sheep when they roamed into other religious fields, not letting them go too far from the good pastures of the Episcopal Church.

Still, Gresham was a good pastor who could allow his sheep some room to roam in pursuit of spiritual nourishment. Christ Church youth were heavily involved in Christian high school clubs. Charlie Cole took a turn as a treasurer of HiY; Kit Swezey, John's younger sister, was recording secretary of the Junior Omega Tri-HiY when she was in the eighth grade, and Suzanne West was president of the Martinsville High School's Omega Tri-HiY as well as the president at the district level.[143] Christ Church's young people also filled many other leadership roles at the high school: Ben Gardner was senior class president; Suzanne West, Ann Whitner, and Alice Yeaman graduated as members of the National Honor Society; student council members included Kit Swezey, Sue Wooldridge, John Swezey,

Duke Sutton, and John Yeaman.[144] In 1959, the last year that the yearbook included a list of the four years of accomplishments of the graduating senior class, Charlie Coles' entry read as follows: "Charlie Cole—Science club 1,2; JV football1,2; Boys Hi-Y 2,Treas 3,4; Key Club 2,3, Pres 4; Varsity Football 3,4; VP Junior Class, Junior Play, Monogram Club 3,4 Wrestling team 3,4; Senior Play, Track team 3,4; Inter club Council 4."

Leadership was part of the genetic makeup of Christ Church members. There is no denying that the adult Christ Church members valued leadership and instilled this attitude in their children. Leadership in the church and the community was given special recognition at Christ Church once a year with the presentation of The Beverly S. Parrish Jr. Christian Leadership Award.

The life of Beverly Parrish Jr. is almost legendary. Born on New Year's Day 1931, he was an active member of Christ Episcopal Church, serving as crucifer for many years. He attained Eagle rank in the Boy Scouts.[145] In high school, he served as president of the Science Club, president of the Virginia Academy of Science, president of the sophomore class, member of Student Council, Glee Club, Latin Club, Dramatic Club, Annual staff, and vice-president of the Spanish Club. He was also an outstanding member of his high school football, basketball, and track teams.

Parrish entered Virginia Tech University and joined the Corps of Cadets, where he served as Cadet Regimental Commander. He was a member of the American Society of Mechanical Engineers, received Outstanding Freshman and Sophomore Awards, the Corps of Engineers' Gold Medal Award, the General Electric Outstanding Senior Engineer Scholarship, and the H. P. Chapman Mechanical Drafting Award. He was 1st Lieutenant in Pershing Rifles, and a member of Tau Beta Pi, Pi Tau Sigma, Omicron Delta Kappa,

Phi Kappa Phi, Scabbard and Blade, German Club, Society of American Military Engineers, and the Cadet Senate. He was a Distinguished Military Student and was elected to *Who's Who Among American College Students.*

Beverly S. Parrish Jr. award plaque

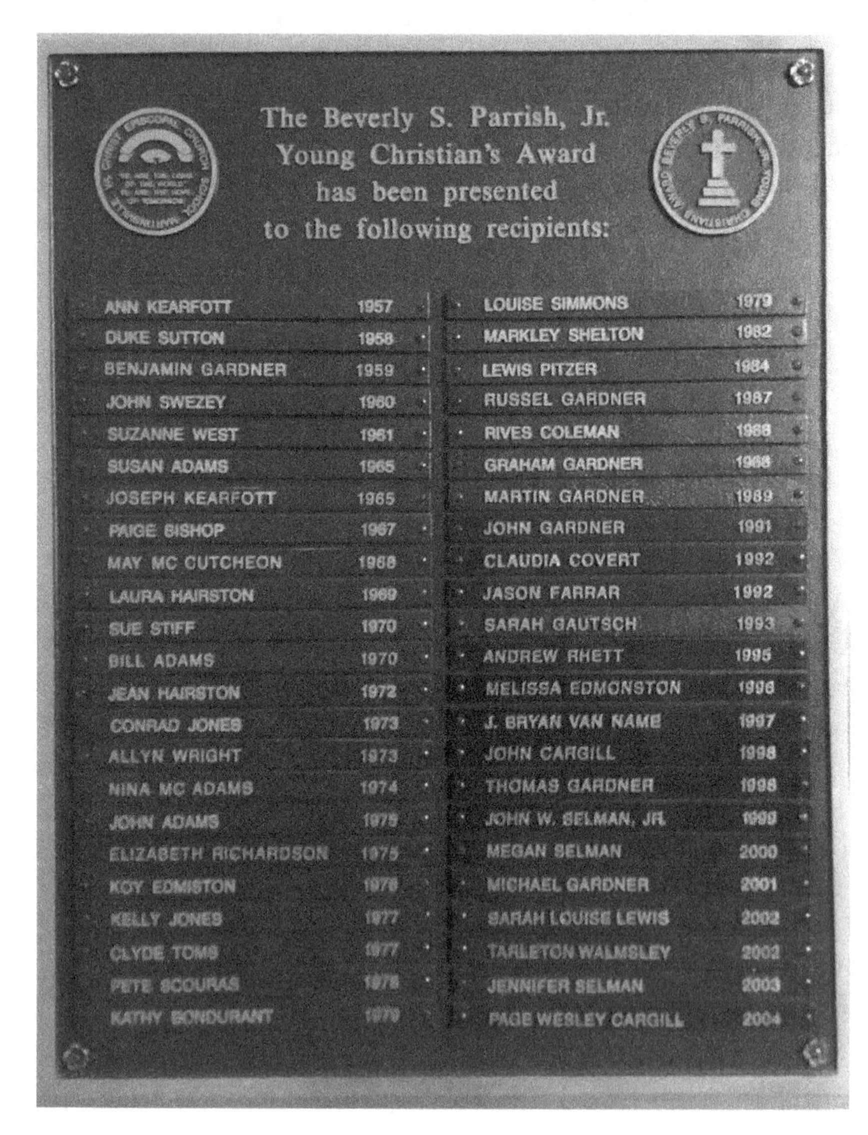

After winning his wings in the United States Air Force, Parrish was assigned as Air Training Officer when the new United States Air Force Academy opened. He was the acting cadet wing commander of the newly established Air Academy and was serving in this capacity when he was killed in a plane crash at Charlotte, North Carolina, on February 11, 1956. Today, for the Virginia Tech Corps of Cadets, the most prized award is the Beverly S. Parrish Award, also known as the Gold Cord, which is presented each year to the top company in the corps.[146] In June of 1956 at Christ Church, it was decided to honor Parrish's memory by recognizing the best qualities of the church's youth with the awarding of the Beverly S. Parrish Jr. Christian Leadership Award. The "Spirit of the Award" is summed up in the tribute made at the time of its first presentation in 1956:

> Beverly S. Parrish Jr. was an active member of Christ Episcopal Church, serving as crucifer for many years. To his family, friends and neighbors he will always be remembered, not only for the honors which he achieved, but for the personal qualities, which he displayed as a boy and a young man. He had a strong sense of duty, he was conscientious in little things and could always be depended on to do his best in any undertaking. He didn't know the meaning of the word 'can't' and was never satisfied unless he did his job well.
>
> Above all, this young man was kind and thoughtful with family and friends. He was a Christian in every sense of the word.[147]

Ann Kearfott was the first to receive the award in 1957. In the summer of 1958, the award went to Duke Sutton. Ben Gardner would follow in 1959, John Swezey in 1960, and Suzanne West in 1961.

Christian youth leaders were rewarded at Christ Church for their Christian virtue, but some of the young people were beginning to question the morality of the leadership role their parents were practicing when it came to racial issues. The controversy in the Episcopal Diocese of Southwestern Virginia was making front-page news and was missed by few. In the 1950s, Christ Church parishioner John Wooldridge was circulation manager for the *Roanoke Times* newspaper in the Martinsville-Henry County area. Even today, Sue Wooldridge Rosser, John's daughter and the 1961 president of the Christ Church Youth Group, remembers the painful embarrassment felt by the church's young people because of the strong and very public segregationist stand of the adult Christ Church leadership[148]—a stand regularly reported in the newspapers. It was the Christ Church vestry's resolution, reprinted in the newspaper, which lit the fuse on the integration issues that exploded at diocesan council, and reverberated through the community. With few exceptions the stand for segregation taken by the vestry would have been reported favorably since most of the major newspapers in Virginia were committed to "Massive Resistance." Gresham heard from a small weekly newspaper editor who told him that he lost thousands of dollars from an advertiser for merely being neutral on the issues of race.[149]

During the summer of 1958, Phil Gresham wrote an article for *The Living Church,* a magazine providing news and commentary for the Episcopal Church.[150] In the first paragraph, he compares what is happening in his diocese to having a bandage ripped off to expose a deep, unhealed wound that is constantly probed and festering. He begins the article by writing, "The Church in the diocese of Southwestern Virginia is violently in newspaper headlines these days." Gresham attempts to inform a national readership of the very real pain that churches in the south are suffering from the segregation-integration battles. "It has ceased to be the pain of Passiontide, and has become the agony of betrayal," he writes.

The Living Church article is remarkable for the insight it affords the reader into the thinking of a young, devoted priest attempting to faithfully live out his Christian duty, his priestly vocation, and his call to a congregation with diverse opinions on the moral issue of their time: racial integration. Gresham writes, "As a priest of the Church, it would be impossible to remain in my parish and not compromise the Gospel unless there were, in some mystical way, light in the darkness." He goes on to quote a favorite author's ideas about crisis in a congregation, "The Rev. C. Kilmer Myers has written in his penetrating *Light the Dark Streets,* 'People must come to understand that a parish not in tension is not, in our day, a Christian parish.'" Gresham comes to believe that the crisis he is facing at Christ Church is "only a different symptom of what the Church has always known," that the Kingdom of God is born from crisis. To his detriment, Gresham's is never able to convince the vestry of his held belief in Myers' proposition.

While troubled by the differences—religious, moral, and social—that Gresham has with members of his congregation he deeply desires to remain a good shepherd for his flock. "In my own parish, we live together, and love each other deeply, despite the tension....Perhaps this agony has drawn us even closer together," he writes. Wounded but hopeful, he provides "a few points of advice for other southern priests who now endure, or will endure this agony." Not surprisingly, his advice has love at its center. "At all times and in all places, love your people," he advises, "Though this is often impossible, yet we, as priests, have been yoked with impossible tasks as our way of life." He reminds the clergy that a good priest is a pastor with a ministry of reconciliation. Gresham believes that a priest's job is, also, to be a prophet, but not at the expense of being a pastor. So, he cautions, "Do not preach loudly about the evils of segregation.... People in agony will not hear what you say." Better, he recommends that the dual ministries of reconciliation and teaching be foremost in a conflicted parish. Gresham desire to hold a conflicted parish together compels him to go so far as to assert that, "To claim that the Churchman who is a segregationist is not a Christian is bigotry."

Gresham's view is that all are sinners and all should be in the church. He knows that within the church there are those who for fear remain mostly silent about their support for racial harmony. "Men must be quiet, or lose business. Women must be quiet, or lose social status." For these intimidated members, the priest is someone to talk to; someone they can trust. A hireling may flee from trouble but the good pastor must protect his flock and risk being wounded. As always with Gresham his willingness to endure pain of conflicted ministry rests with the promise shown by the young people. He tells his fellow clergy to embrace the suffering, the brokenness, of their special ministry, and trust in the future, "It seems that the only sane voice in all this agony is that of our young people, and in them is our deep hope."

Meanwhile, under Gresham's tutelage, the young people were learning that their Episcopal Church needed to break through the barriers that kept the races separated. At church Sunday school, they were being enlightened by Gresham about the injustices of racial segregation. Martinsville's Episcopal Church was teaching a different set of values from what many were getting at home.

Gresham also taught his youth group that it was important that the youth follow their bishop's lead on this moral and justice issue. Bishop Marmion was recognized nationally as well as locally as one of the Episcopal Church's driving forces on the difficult road to racial integration. In Martinsville, the

Christ Church vestry was leading in the opposite direction. In the middle were Christ Church youth, pulled in one direction by their parents and in another by their clergy. To muddle things further, while the bishop and their rector stood against the lay leadership in the dispute over the diocesan youth camping program, Christ Church's young people were often accompanied by their rector at diocesan-sponsored youth functions at a "whites only" hotel at Natural Bridge. In Martinsville, cognitive dissonance was being experienced at an early age. Christian moral leadership by the adult Christians was a garbled mess.

Bishop Marmion made his annual visit to Martinsville in October of 1958. The bishop's visitation is traditionally an important part of any congregation's church year. The bishop meets with the vestry to discuss their concerns and to hear reports on the spiritual as well as the temporal state of the congregation. A church service is held with the bishop presiding and, most often, administering the sacrament of Confirmation. The service is normally followed by a reception honoring the bishop and the new confirmands. If things stretch late into the evening, the vestry arranges for a parishioner to put the bishop up for the night. Virginians take great pride in their reputation for Southern hospitality, but since the tumultuous diocesan council in May, some vestries were finding the courtesy of overnight accommodations for Bishop Marmion difficult or even impossible to arrange. Many church members did not want to be identified with their "integrationist bishop."[151]

The Christ Church vestry meeting of Saturday, October 24, 1958, was called to order at 8 p.m., with Bishop Marmion attending. The vestry minutes mentioned an encouraging report to the bishop of a communicant strength of 378, not including the fifteen persons who were to be confirmed the following day. At his suggestion and with the vestry agreeing, Marmion reviewed the events leading up to the proposal to conduct the youth summer program at Hemlock Haven on a racially integrated basis. "Included in the review and discussion or comments that followed was the action of the Christ Church vestry in its resolution adopted March 18, 1958, opposing the diocesan plan to conduct racially integrated youth conferences."[152] There is no record of how long this special meeting of the vestry lasted or the time it adjourned, but it seems there was a great deal to discuss. No mention is made as to whether the vestry found a bed for the bishop in the home of a willing parishioner.

When the Christ Church vestry convened for its final meeting of the year that December, one of the first orders of business was planning the annual congregational meeting for January 1959. Besides the regularly scheduled election of new vestry members, the focus of this year's meeting would be the "matter of 'Segregation vs. Integration' within the various church activities in the diocese." A team from the special diocesan commission, of which Christ Church's vestryman, Francis T. West, was a member, would be present at the meeting "to present certain information and viewpoints—as well as to obtain from individual parishioners their viewpoints." The results of the team's visit would be part of the commission's assignment to report to the 1959 diocesan council. After receiving the finance committee's proposed budget for 1959, the senior warden, Justice Kennon C. Whittle, submitted the following motion:

> Mr. Chairman and Gentlemen of the Vestry:
>
> Regarding Christ Church's budget for 1959, you will recall that some time ago the Vestry passed a resolution to the effect that we withhold any contributions to the Diocese of Southwestern Virginia, save the Diocesan assessment, until such time as the integration question could be clarified.

In passing this resolution, the Vestry took the position that the segregation-integration question was a political-social question having no connection with religion. My information is that the views of the Vestry in this regard have not changed.

I think both Bishop Marmion and the Rev. Mr. Gresham, our Rector, can be identified as being among those who believe in integration, and as citizens living in a Democracy we respect their personal views.

Knowing that the Vestry of Christ Church does not desire to completely cut our Parish off from the Diocese or the General Church if such can be avoided, several days ago, I requested Mr. Gresham to give me a definition of his interpretation of the term "integration" as he intended it to apply to Christ Church, Martinsville. I now ask him to listen to my interpretation of his remarks and to immediately correct any misunderstanding.

Mr. Gresham, in effect, said that it is not his intention now and never has been his intention to see integration established in Christ Church; that it was not his desire to in any way force integration on the congregation, and that it was his hope that the members of the Church might forget the matter and that we could close ranks and go forward with our work in the Parish in the future as we have in the past. He further stated that [he] had talked with the Bishop and that he could assure us that the Bishop felt as he did.

In regard to Hemlock Haven, the Rector said that a study commission had been appointed and would make a report to the Executive Board of the Diocese, which Board would refer the findings of the Commission to the next meeting of the Council of the Diocese, and if the Diocese determined against the integration of the Youth

> Conference then, in that event, the matter would be settled according to the views of the Vestry of Christ Church; that if on the other hand, the Council voted to conduct an integrated Youth Conference then, of course, it would be entirely up to the parents of children to say whether or not their children should attend such an integrated conference.
>
> The above covered the discussion between us.
>
> In view of this clarification of the unfortunate controversy, which has arisen in our Parish, and with good will toward all men and all races of men, I move that we resolve to the askings of our Diocese for the year 1959, with the hope and prayer that any differences existing between us be resolved and we go forward with Christ's work in the future as we have tried to do in the past.

Senior Warden Whittle's motion passed and with it the budget was approved after two amendments: 1.) Francis West asked that "the Vestry comply with all Diocesan askings except the item headed "Builders for Christ," in the sum of $876.00"; and 2.) after some discussion the rector's travel allowance was raised to $600.00 per year. It is not clear why West objected to the "Builders" capital campaign program, although he may have objected because some of the money for this program was used to pay the note for Hemlock Haven.[153]

15

Movers & Shakers

In their final meeting of 1958, the vestry of Christ Church affirmed their stand on one of the hottest controversies of their day: whether political-social questions can be disconnected from religion and vice versa. Six decades later, the heat that question generates has not abated, but only grown. Who gets to decide—the church, the courts, the politicians or the individual—on matters of race, abortion, end of life, gender identification, alternate lifestyles, and religious expression is still not settled. Opinions on the correct answer still divide communities. The leadership of Christ Episcopal Church was also the leadership of Martinsville, so it was naturally assumed by them that they knew what was best for their community, religious, and civil. The people of Martinsville seemed to agree.

Today, enshrined on a paneled wall of the City Council room on the second floor of the municipal building are the pictures of the mayors of Martinsville. Christ Church is impressively well represented: members Tom Burch, Charles Hart, Fred Woodson, Francis West, and William Cole all had the honor of being called "Mister Mayor" by their fellow parishioners and neighbors. One more Christ Church member of note is remembered in the foyer of city hall for his service to Martinsville. Near the main entrance is a dedication to W. H. Yeaman, who for thirty-seven years served as city clerk. The tenacious Yeaman spent an unbelievable fifty years as organist at Christ Church and was the long-time secretary of the vestry.

On Sunday mornings in 1958, the polished pews of Christ Church were populated with the families of politicians and government officials. Christ Church Sunday morning worship also attracted the families of many prominent businessmen. A host of the DuPont plant executives attended, as did the top management of furniture manufacturing mainstays Hooker, American, and Bassett. The families who owned the city's independent gas company and the home heating oil company worshipped at Christ Church. These movers and shakers of business and politics elected and reelected each other to the Christ Church vestry. A closer look at two of these members, Francis T. West and Kennon C. Whittle, will be helpful in understanding how it was.

In the annals of Christ Church, few men can claim more influence in his community or his church than did Francis T. West Sr. In his slim volume *Magnet,* Ralph C. Lester introduces Francis Thomas West Sr. as a "mover and shaker." While Justice Kennon Whittle was known to be a man of moderate temperament whose practiced sense of fairness caused him to pursue concord in the face of conflict,[154] the same cannot be said for Whittle's fellow Christ Church vestryman, Francis T. West, who was never afraid to be the center of attention—and contention. Like Whittle, West was deeply devoted to Christ Episcopal Church. The Rev. Phil Gresham had West licensed as a lay reader in 1960 while West served on the vestry. West also served numerous times as a delegate or alternate for Christ Church to the diocesan council and was elected by that body as a deputy to the 1961 Episcopal Church General Convention, the church's national legislative body, which meets every three years.

West's talents for organization and public speaking helped make him the prosperous owner of West Window Company. They also made him a formidable, high-profile opponent of racial integration. In 1962, when 17-year-old Ruth Hazel Adams was the first black student to complete admission procedures for the Patrick Henry Branch of the University of Virginia, it was West who spoke to Roanoke TV station WSLS for the eleven-man governing board of that branch and accused the university of breaking its word to them that the school would not be integrated. The *New York Times* printed three articles about this episode. The last account reported that Adams quit the university after attending class for a single day. As a vehement segregationist, West's picture and quotes often appeared in newspaper articles about the disputes over the diocesan youth summer program. He remained a vocal leader in opposing Bishop Marmion's policy to integrate Hemlock Haven. Behind the scenes, he corresponded with like-minded churchmen whom he saw as partners in this "struggle." In one letter he wrote:

> December 1, 1962
> C O N F I D E N T I A L
>
> My dear friends—about 150 of you…on of [sic] more in each of our churches…except eighteen:
>
> Five grueling years of Hemlock Haven have been wearing. Segregation by sex at our conference center will be an established fact next summer. Threatened Executive Board action by fiat has frustrated and angered. Arbitrary and arrogant parliamentary rulings and procedures have embittered. In five years, we have only gained 128 communicants; a meager rise of only 1 1/2%. Yet the assessment has increase 65%—"asking" 45%.
>
> SHALL WE QUIT?…I, for one, cannot; nor, I believe, can you. But, if we are to impede the on-rushing tide of

liberalism and clerical domination in our beloved diocese, I've got to work harder and so have you. Otherwise, what are now utterances by our ecclesiastical leaders through the left-leaning "Virginia Council on Human Relations" could become the official voice of the diocese. I refer to this organization's endorsement of the federal government's decree that there must be integrated housing in the event of mortgage loans have even a remote federal identity—FHA, GI, etc. Apathy on our part also will allow (the Chancellor has already so stated) the Executive Board to change the segregation by sex policy at its discretion. Even now, difficulty is seen by the clergy in enticing high school boys and girls to attend conferences; in the absence of the other sex.

We have to remember that two things are absolute and basic if our group is to be effective. Number one—conservatives must be elected to vestries. Number two—vestries must then elect conservatives to Council. VESTRY CONSIDERATION AND GROUNDWORK MUST START NOW! New members are usually elected in December and January.

Our group has had several problems, which should be corrected. Each letter I've circulated, invariably has fallen into the hands of one or more of the clergy at Evans House. Largely, I think this has been accidental; but it should stop. Of course, if you are not in agreement with the purpose of our group and don't wish to keep our matters with the confidence of concerned laymen of like thinking, so state, and I won't bother you with further mailings. Too, there are those with influence among us who are perhaps not making this influence felt. Although there are some churches that we don't even have a "foot in the door," there are others, where we are well represented, that from time to time elect liberal delegates to Council. For example, we had about sixty of our persuasion at Lexington—three Councils ago—only to drop to under fifty last May at Roanoke.

To make further plans I should know just how many of you (I sincerely hope all) will continue to help in the struggle. Right now, will you please write me your intentions? I've got a pretty thick skin so don't hesitate to verbalize any criticisms you may have. To correctly tabulate, may I hear from each of you—even if you "want out." Separately, I am enclosing a "score sheet" showing churches whose delegates are consistently against us; also showing churches with a vote or two against us, but where rather immediate improvement could be made. In your response, please indicate where you think you may be of help, either in your own church or a neighboring one. Also, advise if you think I've erred in classifying.

Sincerely,
Francis T. West[155]

Along with his letter was a "score sheet" analysis based on the Forty-third Annual Council of the Diocese of Southwestern Virginia. It listed, in group A, twenty-seven "against us" votes that included the chancellor and the historiographer. An asterisk was placed next to the names of four of the churches with a note that these were "Colored Churches." Group B was explained as "Delegates from the following churches did not attend Council; most of whom probably would have voted with our group." Five churches were listed in group B. Above the column that made up Group C was the explanation, "Churches below either sent split delegations (one with us—one against) or totally opposed to our position." Nine churches were listed in Group C. The "Score Sheet" included two "observations" at the bottom of the page:

> OBSERVATION #1. Prospects are not promising in changing many of the solid 27 (A) "Against" votes. Other than at St. John's Bedford and Hot Springs, we don't even have a contact. Perhaps some of your efforts may change this.
>
> OBSERVATION #2. Classifications B and C should be our primary concern. Here we have the contacts—directly or neighboring. With proper effort we should at least see that twelve out of the fourteen delegates are of our persuasion and that they attend future Councils. Add twelve to our already solid core of about fifty and our voice can and will be effective.

West put great effort into leading a cabal that worked against Bishop Marmion and the forces of integration in the Diocese of Southwestern Virginia. Whether you were for or against his positions, there was no denying that he could be a formidable opponent or capable ally. West saw himself as a dedicated member of the resistance against the corrupting forces of social change in his church and in his white culture. His public pronouncements and behind-the-scenes maneuvering made West a champion of racial segregation for many at Christ Church Martinsville and only added to his standing in the community.

West was certainly considered a pillar of the community at Christ Episcopal Church, serving in numerous leadership roles on both sides of the altar rail, from licensed lay reader to vestryman. Still, in a hierarchical church such as the Episcopal Church where leadership is formally recognized and titled, the congregation's chief lay minister is its senior warden. And for 14 years in the 1950s and the 1960s that title belonged to Virginia Supreme Court Justice Kennon Caithness Whittle.

The Whittle family is rooted deeply in the history and the culture of Virginia. Kennon Whittle's father, Stafford Gorman

Whittle, attended Washington and Lee University during the period when the Confederate hero, Gen. Robert E. Lee, was president of the institution. Judge E. J. Harvey remarked about Lee's influence on Stafford Whittle, "There is no doubt that he imbibed from that great patriot, and exponent of duty, many of the principles which characterized his course of life."[156] Kennon, who followed his father into the practice of law, then to the bench, and, like his father, became a justice of the state Supreme Court of Appeals, undoubtedly adopted much of his father's sense of duty and his life principles. Kennon took the oath of office for the Supreme Court fifty years to the month after his father had been sworn in to the same bench. The chief justice administering the oath referred to Kennon as "a worthy son of a noble sire."[157]

Justice Kennon Whittle was the epitome of the paradox that was the Virginian of religious conviction and high principles yet deeply and thoroughly immersed in the Southern ethos of white privilege in the 1950s. Years before the diocesan battle over Hemlock Haven the complexity of this man and his times were vividly on display in the shocking trial of the "Martinsville Seven."

On January 8, 1949, Ruby Stroud Flood, a 32-year-old white resident of Martinsville, accused seven black men of raping her "10 or 12 times." The brutal nature of the crime shocked the community. It took only a couple of days for local authorities to arrest all of the suspects and obtain confessions from each of them. At the request of the defense attorneys, the defendants were each to be tried separately.[158] All of the trials were assigned to the courtroom presided over by Judge Kennon Whittle.

In Virginia courts at the time of the trial of the "Martinsville Seven," a conviction for violent rape carried the possibility of the death penalty. The commonwealth had begun using the electric chair for executions in 1908. By 1949, all 45 men executed for rape in Virginia were African-Americans convicted of attacking white women. Not all convicted black men survived long enough to make it to the executioner in the states that made up the old Confederacy. In the strict, white, patriarchal Southern tradition, the honor of a white woman was to be highly regarded and vigorously defended. A perceived white male duty often shockingly upheld was death—often gruesome—by a lynch mob if the accused rapist was a black man. As Eric Walter Rise notes, in his *The Martinsville Seven and Southern Justice,* it might seem praiseworthy that Virginia was second only to North Carolina for having the fewest lynchings of blacks until one realizes that only three states executed more blacks for rape than Virginia.[159]

A black defendant accused of rape in the Commonwealth of Virginia could be assumed to be a target for a lynch mob. Rise relates how Judge Whittle, concurring with the police's assessment of the risk to the seven accused's safety, "ordered that they remain jailed outside Henry County 'in order that there would be no unfortunate happening in the city.'" Whittle "claimed he did not fear any mob violence but he insisted that the state had a responsibility 'to protect these men from any trouble that might happen.'" As Whittle would later recall, "God knows we didn't want anything to happen in the way of a lynching."[160]

The defense attorneys for the Seven asked for a change of venue, contending that "highly inflammatory" pretrial publicity in Martinsville precluded a fair hearing for the accused. Twenty-five witnesses were called to the stand in support of the defense's motion. The first witness called was Christ Church parishioner and Commonwealth's Attorney for Henry County—the county's prosecutor—Cary J. Randolph. As the *Martinsville Bulletin* reported it: "Asked if he thought the defendants could get a fair trial here (in Martinsville), he replied it depended on the juror. He said he believed most people have made up their minds that the men are guilty but he said he did not think there is any prejudice against the defendants as individuals. He said any prejudice was 'against the nature of the crime.'" Cary went on to testify that he thought it possible to find twelve men to decide the case on the evidence although "it would be a difficult task." Another witness from Christ Church to take the stand in the pretrial hearing was none other than its rector, the Rev. Charles Fishburne. Christ Church's rector did not advance the cause of the defense or the prosecution but simply stated that he did not know enough about the case "to say if they (the defendants) can be given a fair trial." Probably more people agreed with the taxicab driver who told the court, "I guess they could get a fair trial...People think they are guilty because they confessed."[161]

The day after the hearing for change of venue Judge Whittle ruled against the motion for a change. As the trial sped forward to its statistically predictable conclusion, Whittle's stated faith in his community to conduct a fair trial was unwavering. The *Bulletin* reported the Judge's opening remarks: "The public in this community should be congratulated upon the way they have conducted themselves in this matter. The press should be congratulated on the way it has handled the news of this unfortunate thing." The judge said he believed he could ensure fairness in his court and went on to warn that he would "permit strenuous examination of any panel that is brought here for trial and will see that any juror will be free from prejudice..."[162]

There were six capital trials for the seven men; two defendants elected to be tried together. The trials were held back-to-back, none of them lasting more than a day.[163] Prospective jurors in each trial included some blacks, but all 72 jurors selected to decide the cases were white; many of the black jurors were excused because they opposed the death penalty.

The first trial was typical of the rest. The jury required only thirty minutes and one ballot to find the defendant guilty and sentence him to die in the electric chair.[164] In the end, all of the juries convicted the defendants, and all were recommended for the death penalty. Four men were electrocuted on February 2, 1951, and three were electrocuted three days later.

Some judged the Martinsville Seven trial as a "Legal Lynching." That judgment overlooks Whittle's lifelong personal dedication to the rule of law, albeit prejudicial laws, and his stated efforts regarding the need for fairness in court.[165] Before the trials began Whittle put all of the attorneys on notice of their "duty as lawyers to see that these defendants receive a fair and impartial trial and that a true verdict be rendered in each case in accordance with the law and evidence," and he adjured the attorneys to "play fairly with the Court." He warned the attorneys to downplay the racial overtones of the case. Addressing the defense counsel, he asked the more experienced members of the defense team to assist the younger attorneys in the trial of their clients.[166] Whittle's instructions to the attorneys were hardly the stuff of a judge inciting a legal lynching, granted his concern seemed more bent toward keeping peace in the community than concern for the rights of the defendants. His warning, as recounted in the *Martinsville Bulletin*, to both the prosecution and the defense again voiced his faith in his community: "I here and now admonish you that this case must and will be tried in such a way as not to disturb the kindly feeling now locally existing between the races. It must be tried as though both parties were members of the same race. I will not have it otherwise."

The judge continued that a rape trial is always "unfortunate" for the community. It would have been best had Whittle stopped there. Still, the judge seemed helpless to completely throw off a lifetime of white Southern values. He benefitted neither himself, the black defendants, nor a racially mixed community by suggesting in regard to the alleged rapes and the trial that "if possible, it is made even more regrettable due to the fact that these seven negroes are charged with the rape of a white woman."[167]

In Virginia, where only African-Americans had ever been executed for rape, it must have struck the black spectators in the courtroom as extreme irony to hear Whittle instruct the jury that Virginia law prohibited any racial distinctions when determining punishment. In accepting the juries' recommendation for the death penalty for the convicted, Judge Whittle "allowed more than sixty days to give them an opportunity to exhaust their legal appeals, commenting, 'If errors have been made I pray God they may be corrected.'"[168] The appeals were quick in coming on behalf of all of the convicted for all six trials. The appeals cited "numerous errors of law" by the circuit court, including Judge Whittle's refusal for change of venue, plus the charge that holding the cases on practically successive days denied the accused due process.[169] During the appeals process, author Eric Rise notes, the state argued that the convictions be upheld, citing among other points "the impeccable conduct of Judge Whittle."[170] In denying the appeal of the Martinsville Seven, the appellate judge commended Judge Whittle for the "exemplary manner in which [he] presided over and supervised the conduct of the cases," adding that his behavior "could well serve as a model for trial judges throughout the Commonwealth."[171]

Besides the legal appeal, there was a growing appeal to the public that questioned the fairness of the death sentence for seven men in a racially charged rape trial. Upholding the sentences and the fairness of the trials were editorial opinions like that of the *Danville Register,* which called the crime "unequalled in heinousness in the recent annals of the judicial circuit in which it occurred."[172] Others believed that the sentences were a throwback to the days of slavery when an antebellum statute expressly reserved the death penalty for rape for convicted negroes.[173] The *Richmond African-American* argued, "The death penalty for criminal assault in Virginia is reserved for Colored men only and has never been applied to a white man in the State's history."[174] The sentencing only of blacks to death for rape was proof, the newspaper said, that the "statutes have been applied and administered by public authority with an evil eye and an unequal hand so as to make unjust and illegal discrimination between persons in similar circumstances." The NAACP entered the fray on behalf of the defendants and petitioned the United States Supreme Court to review the case. In their petition to the Court they wrote, "It is clear that the death penalty for rape or attempted rape is now and always has been in Virginia reserved solely for Negroes convicted of rape upon white women. White men have always had an immunity from such penalty."[175] The Supreme Court refused to review the case in a writ of certiorari.[176]

The lack of regard for the racial imbalance of those executed for rape in Virginia hangs over the trials of the Martinsville Seven, and it cannot be disregarded. Sixty years after the trial of the Martinsville Seven the *Richmond Times-Dispatch* asked Washington and Lee University law professor David Bruck to comment on the trial and the fact that all 45 men executed for rape in Virginia between 1908 and 1951 were African-American. Brock told the state's paper of record, that even if the trials were fair and the men guilty, "the idea that you could have a 45-to-nothing ratio and that does not prove anything... tells you that this was simply a judicial system that was not prepared to do the right thing."[177]

President Lyndon B. Johnson famously said, "Doing what's right isn't the problem. It is knowing what's right." While Johnson's point is well taken, it is also true that often knowing what is right is obvious and ignoring that fact is a mark of cowardice, malice, or a combination of both. The level of systemic ignorance, systemic cowardice or systemic malice that allowed the Virginia judicial system to parcel out justice so radically disparate at the trials of white and black defendants is obvious and morally indefensible. It is difficult not to conclude that those who made up the judicial system could have and should have done better.

Judge Whittle's pedigree along with his reputation in prominent trials including the "Martinsville Seven" helped to elevate him to the highest judicial realms in Virginia. His stature in the community was not lost on the members of Christ Church, who repeatedly elected him to the vestry and made him its senior warden. Like his fellow vestryman Francis West, he probably did not question the prominence he enjoyed in church and white society. While both men had argued in favor of disconnecting political-social questions from religion, they were highly involved in both of those spheres and, given the positions they held, believed themselves to be arbiters of what was right in both realms. And that too was just part of "the way it was."

Of course, not everyone agreed with this state of affairs. Chief among the dissenters were Gresham's youth group at Christ Church, who had a different take on what was right and who gets to decide. As the decade of the 1950s reached its final year, those young people were leaning in to the rebellious decade of the '60s, just a year away. In 1959, Christ Church's youth would start to question authority.

16

A Gift for the Bishop

Throughout any given year, Christ Church's youth group kept busy with gatherings and special events. Like most teenagers then and now, they kept their calendar in sync with the rhythm of the school year. As members of a church youth group, they also moved to the beat of the church's liturgical calendar. Easter, the celebration of Jesus Christ's triumph over death, is the highest of holy days on the Christian calendar, and in 1959 that central Christian feast day arrived early, Sunday March 29.[178]

In preparation for its major feast day, the church subjects itself to a penitential season of self-discipline, the forty days of Lent beginning on Ash Wednesday. In predominantly Roman Catholic cities such as Rio de Janeiro or New Orleans, the day before Ash Wednesday, known as Fat Tuesday or Mardi Gras, is a day of excess before the weeks of Lenten fasting. Abstaining from meat on Fridays is a common Lenten practice. Fat Tuesday festivities, such as Carnivale, give the celebrants an opportunity to say farewell to meat, or as others would have it, a time to say goodbye for forty days to the enjoyment of the things of the flesh.[179] In the English church, the day before Ash Wednesday has traditionally been marked with considerably less exuberance than the parade floats and half-naked samba dancers of Carnivale: The day before Ash Wednesday, Shrove Tuesday, was traditionally the day to confess one's sins, to be shriven, the Old English term and etiological origin for Shrove Tuesday. It was also considered the last chance to consume delicacies such as butter, sugar, and milk before the Lenten season of fasting and abstinence. In 1959, Ash Wednesday, dependent on the date of Easter, fell rather early for the season, February 11. For February 10, the Christ Church Youth Group planned their biggest fund raiser of the year, the Shrove Tuesday pancake supper.

Both John Swezey and Sue Wooldridge Rosser used the same word to describe the pancake suppers of their youth: "Huge!"[180] "We would have fifteen to twenty teens cooking and serving," Swezey remembered, "There would be a line of hungry customers out the door." Rosser agreed, "Everybody came to the Shrove Tuesday pancake supper." Memories differed about who started the suppers. Swezey gave the credit to Gresham, while Rosser remembers attending them before his arrival. However, there is no argument that they were the biggest and best during the Gresham years. And the increase in enthusiasm for the pancake suppers was attributed to the motivation behind the effort: The money raised by the youth group was dedicated to a gift for the bishop, a crozier.

The word *Episcopal* derives from the Greek word "episkopos"—translated bishop, but literally, overseer, understood to be the one who oversees or shepherds the flock. The hierarchy of authority in the Episcopal Church resides with the bishop of the diocese. St. Ignatius of Antioch, who was born about the time that Jesus died, was one of the first bishops in succession from the twelve apostles, the original bishops. It is St. Ignatius who is credited with placing bishops at the functional center of the church, writing, "Where the bishop is, there let the people be, as where Jesus is, there is the catholic church."[181] The Rev. Philip Gresham would have agreed with St. Ignatius enthusiastically. The priest as pastor guides his congregational flock under the authority of the diocese's chief pastor, the bishop. This connection between a bishop and his priest is clearly manifested in the rite of the ordination of a priest. In the 1928 Book of Common Prayer in use at the time of his ordination, Gresham swore to reverently obey his bishop, "following with a glad mind and will" his bishop's "godly admonitions" and submitting himself to his bishop's "godly judgements."[182]

An ancient symbol of the bishop's authority was a shepherd's crook—in church parlance, a crozier. However, most of Christ Church's members would not have known a crozier from a croissant. For this lack of knowledge, they could blame their local history. Many of the first Anglican priests in Virginia were from the Puritan wing of the Church of England. As such, they rejected much of the ritual and trappings of worship that they considered Roman Catholic excesses.[183] In the low church Diocese of Southwestern Virginia, the bishop did not carry a crozier, nor had the diocese ever owned one.

Philip Gresham did not hold to the traditional Virginia style of low churchmanship, preferring instead the manner and ceremony of high church Anglo-Catholicism. One Christ Church Sunday school teacher wrote a friend, "I made some reference during the evening to him as 'Preacher,' and man, he really let me have it (both barrels)...He really preferred to be called Father and had inclinations of high church."[184]

The church, like the military, has its own language, its own way of doing things, and Gresham delighted in "churchiness." Until Gresham arrived, the room under the nave of the church was simply the church basement. Gresham trained everyone to use the traditional ecclesiastical term, "undercroft," for that space.[185] One liturgical ceremony he particularly favored was the procession. At Christ Episcopal Church, most services began with organ swells and the congregation standing and singing as the liturgical leaders entered the nave of the church. The procession would be led by a large brass processional cross carried high and lifted up by a crucifer dressed in red cassock, white surplice, and white linen gloves that prevented the natural oils in his hands from marring the brass. The crucifer was flanked by flag bearers vested in black cassock, white surplice, and white linen gloves, carrying the flags of the United States and the Episcopal Church. Next in procession was the adult choir; both men and women dressed in black cassock and white cotta. The women were additionally vested with white collars with large black bow and, since all women were required to wear hats in church, black mortar boards. On special occasions, the adult choir would be preceded by the youth choir, mostly and often exclusively young girls, dressed in red cassock and white cotta. Before Gresham arrived, the youth choir was simply designated as the youth choir. Gresham renamed it "the Canterbury choir," and so the traditional square Canterbury caps in red were purchased for the girls in the choir to match their cassocks. At the end of the procession, the liturgical place of honor, was the ordained celebrant, Gresham, vested in cassock, surplice, and stole. Stripped of its pomp, the procession is simply a means for getting the priest, altar servers, and the choir to their seats in the church.

The longstanding custom for Christ Church was to process, at the beginning of the service, down the aisle on the Gospel side of the nave to the chancel with the choir to take their place in the choir stalls while the celebrant and servers made their way to the altar. Simple and effective. However, that was too short a walk for Gresham's liking. Rather than permitting everyone in the procession to take their seats once they reached the front of the church, Gresham's procession would pass the altar rail and turn up the aisle on the Epistle side and proceed to the back of the church. At the door, the crucifer would turn and lead the procession through the narrow space between the back wall and the last pew until they reached the Gospel side aisle, where they would turn again to retrace their steps to the chancel, choir stalls, and altar to finish the entrance procession. When challenged by a member to explain his reasons for changing the simple entrance used in the past and for adding the long circuitous route, Gresham smiled broadly and said, "I love a parade!"[186] Later, Gresham would request the purchase of the church's first processional torches to add to the pomp.

Torches, flags, processional crosses, choirs dressed in colorful vestments were, to the mind of Gresham, all necessary components of doing church the right way. It is fair speculation that Gresham was pained by the site of the bishop, at his annual visitation, entering Christ Church unaccompanied by the ancient symbol of his office, his crozier. While there is no record of who suggested that the Christ Church youth group buy a crozier as a gift for the bishop, it is more than probable that the idea came from Gresham. "I didn't know a crozier from a 'dozer and neither did anyone," Swezey recalls. "Gresham said that the bishop doesn't have one." Somehow, it seems likely, Gresham convinced the youth that getting the bishop a crozier was a worthy project.

The first mention of the use of the Shrove Tuesday pancake supper as a fundraiser for the bishop's crozier was in the youth report for 1957. That year Shrove Tuesday was just a few months before the diocese purchased Hemlock Haven and a year before the Christ Church vestry publicly opposed their bishop's plan for the integration of the camp. The Christ Church youth group originally made the decision to buy a crozier simply as a generous gift to their bishop. But over the next few years the crozier became much more.

"It was a real peace offering," Sue Wooldridge Rosser states with no hesitation. By 1959, the feeling among the Christ Church young people was that their adult leadership had become "a real embarrassment" for the way they reacted to the proposed integration of Hemlock Haven. After Christ Church's 1959 annual meeting, the gift became the vehicle for the youth group to distance themselves from the position of their parish's adult leaders and to demonstrate their support for their bishop and his stand on racial integration.

The transition from gift to peace offering had its genesis at the 1959 annual parish meeting in January of that year. Francis West had briefed the vestry at their December 1958 meeting that the congregation would be invited to air their views on the proposed integration of Hemlock Haven summer youth conferences at the 1959 parish meeting. A group from the Diocesan Study Committee, of which West was a member, would make a presentation at the January annual meeting and then receive comments from members of the congregation. The feedback from Christ Church would then become part of the committee's report to the Diocesan Executive Board in advance of the 1959 diocesan council. The Christ Church youth group felt strongly that they should have a voice in the making of the policy for the camp, so they asked for their comment to be heard. Knowing that their vestrymen were leaders in the faction to keep the youth camp racially segregated, they saw the annual meeting as their opportunity to record their disagreement with that policy. For a few of the youth this meant public opposition to their parents.

Christ Church had a rector who was heavily involved in youth work in all of it phases. Phil Gresham was diocesan youth director and an unsurprising favorite pick when clergy sponsors were needed for diocesan youth events. Christ Church was among the largest youth groups in the diocese with an outsize presence at diocesan gatherings. They had hosted the youth convocation in 1957, and three of its members were elected officers by their peers: Ruth Drewry as president, Duke Sutton as parliamentarian, and Chauncy Drewry as secretary/treasurer. Back at home, Gresham regularly attended the Sunday night get-togethers in the church undercroft. Under Gresham's guidance and direction, Christ Church's youth crafted their thoughts and feelings about the Hemlock Haven controversy into a written "Manifesto" that would be presented at the annual meeting.

The use of the term manifesto for the youth group statement was itself controversial; it was a loaded term from racial politics. Two years after the Supreme Court ordered the integration of the nation's schools in *Brown v. Board of Education,* a group of nineteen United States senators and seventy-seven members of the House of Representatives, including the entire Virginia delegation, issued a statement condemning that ruling. The document called the 1954 *Brown* decision "a clear abuse of judicial power" and encouraged states to resist implementing its mandates. Officially entitled "The Declaration of Constitutional Principles," it is commonly referred to as "The Southern Manifesto."

The Christ Church youth group would have its own manifesto, but with a decidedly different point of view. "Basically, it said, 'Can't we all just get along,'" John Swezey remembers. Although the manifesto is lost, it is safe to believe that the sentiments of both the rector and the bishop regarding race relations were being taught to and absorbed by the Christ Church youth. Gresham had the reputation as the type of teacher who would challenge his students to "hash out" moral and ethical situations rather than just accept the status quo. As many as eight of Christ Church's young people had informed Gresham that they had planned to take part in last summer's integrated camp at Hemlock Haven despite the vestry's advice against attending. In direct opposition to their vestry's stated position the youth group manifesto would call for racial equality as a response to the Christian Gospel.

Once the manifesto was produced, it fell to the president of the youth group, Charlie Cole, to present it at the annual meeting. The big problem for Charlie was that his father, the vestryman, Sunday school teacher, and future mayor of Martinsville, was opposed to the racial integration the manifesto championed. "My father and Francis West were segregationists who would never send their children to an integrated youth camp," Charlie remembers. When he heard that Charlie would be the spokesperson for the youth group, the senior Cole absolutely forbade his son to read the manifesto at the annual meeting. The memory of that opportunity missed is still painful for Charlie Cole more than five decades later, but he tries to be philosophical about how it was growing up in the 1950s. "In those days," Cole said, "we did what our father told us to do." With great reluctance Charlie informed Gresham that he had been forbidden by his father to read the youth manifesto at the annual meeting. Since the president of the youth group was forced to withdraw, Gresham needed a leader that both the youth group and the adults of the congregation would immediately respect. Gresham chose Charlie Cole's classmate and the most recent winner of the Beverly Parrish award, high school senior Duke Sutton.

By the day of the 1959 annual meeting, many of the adult parishioners were aware of the gist of the youth manifesto, and they were not happy. There are no extant copies, but we have strong evidence of what it may have contained. Some of that evidence is contained in the Diocesan House of Young Churchmen's report to the 1960 diocesan council. It stated that at the winter youth conference a straw vote was taken, and by a 3 to 1 majority, the young people attending said "they would attend youth conferences on a non-segregated basis." Speaking for the youth of the diocese, the president of the Young Churchmen, Joseph Straub, told the council that young Episcopalians "want an opportunity for broader fellowship with all people."[188]

We know that Gresham attended the winter conferences in 1959 and 1960 along with some of the Christ Church youth. It is more than likely that the document that Sutton read at the Christ Church annual meeting in 1959 contained many of the same elements of Straub's address and may have been its precursor. When it came time for the youth group report at Christ Church's annual meeting, the adults listened politely to Duke Sutton, but there was broad murmuring of disapproval when he finished. The youth of Christ Church had publicly taken a position directly opposed to the established position of their parents, their vestry, and the lay leaders of the diocese on the hot topic of racial integration. In a small town like Martinsville, a former youth group member recalled "People cared what their neighbor thought and reputations were tightly guarded."

In Virginia in 1959, children who openly opposed their parents were presumed to be the product of some flaw in their family life. As tension slowly percolated through the undercroft, Cary Randolph—attorney, licensed lay reader, and active churchman—took the floor of the meeting. In a sanguine tone, he began by congratulating Sutton and the Christ Church youth for having an interest in the current events of the church and society. The fine young people of the youth group were the future of the church. But for now, he advised that the young people focus on their studies, on doing well in school, and allow the adults to handle these difficult problems with their many repercussions that the youth could not possibly understand.[189] When Randolph finished his comments, the adults vigorously applauded their agreement. After having their opinion so soundly dismissed, the demoralized and despondent youth left the adults to their meeting.

The parents of Christ Church saw themselves as responsible leaders of the community who raised their children to follow in their footsteps. They held up the courageous example of one of their own, Beverly Parrish, as a model for the youth of the congregation "for the personal qualities which he displayed...a Christian in every sense of the word." Sadly, the adults of the congregation did not recognize their own cognitive dissonance that encouraged Christian virtues in their children but discouraged it when those qualities manifested themselves at inopportune times on inconvenient issues. As Bishop Heath Light pointed out many years later, it is hard to reconcile how the vehement racist attitudes existed in a church that regularly invited the era's greatest Christian theologians to speak at its Laymen's League. When it comes to racism, labeling this thinking merely as hypocrisy does not do justice to its spiritual dimension. Perhaps Jesus' words to his disciples better fit the situation: "With them indeed is fulfilled the prophecy of Isaiah which says: 'You shall indeed hear but never understand, and you shall indeed see but never perceive.'"[190] One thing is for certain: After the annual meeting of 1959, the bishop's gift took on new importance and new meaning for the Christ Church youth group.

17

Race is the Issue

The prominence of the Episcopal Church in 1950s Virginia is evidenced by the fact that the results of the meetings of the Executive Board of the Diocese of Southwestern Virginia were widely, even nationally reported. On February 26, 1959, an AP report ran under the headline "EPISCOPALIANS SPLIT ON RACIAL MIXING."[191] The news service went on to report the evaluation given to the executive board by the study commission members, whom the diocesan council had charged with developing a policy on race relations for programs at the diocesan camp and conference center at Hemlock Haven in advance of the 1959 diocesan council meeting. What the board received were two reports from a committee divided 11 to 8 "because the clergymen and lay leaders could not agree on a race policy."[192] The majority report signed by "mostly laymen" recommended what was described as "separate but equal facilities."[193] The policy would allow for certain periods at Hemlock Haven for white communicants and certain periods for negro communicants. The minority report signed by eight "mostly" clergy committeemen proposed a "local option plan by which each parish could reserve a certain time for use of the lodge for conferences." Once again, a compromise position was floated by the minority clergy group to integrate the races but segregate by gender for certain age groups. Once again, this "Perennial Resolution" died on the vine. For the executive board, two reports were almost worse than none. "After both reports were rejected," the AP reported, "the Rev. Wilfred Roach, Grace Church Radford, moved that the matter be referred back to the commission for 'further study.' The Rev. Roach's motion carried unanimously." The hope that the executive board held out for avoiding a repeat of the contentious 1958 council meeting was manifestly fading.

Around the diocese, vestries were making their preparations for the April annual council, to be held at St. Paul's Church in Lynchburg. After the Christ Church vestry reelected Justice Kennon Whittle as senior warden and Clarence Kearfott as junior warden at its February 4 meeting, they also elected without comment or opposition Kearfott and Francis West as delegates to the annual Diocesan Council. Forty miles north at Trinity Episcopal Church in Rocky Mount, things did not go as smoothly. After years of struggling, the congregation was preparing to ask the diocesan council for a change from mission status to that of self-supporting parish, a momentous step in the life of a church. The Diocesan Council would be asked to recognize that Trinity Church had established sufficient membership and financial strength to secure its survival without the direct assistance of the diocese. The Trinity Church vestry would assume direct control of the parish's finances. The priest leading the congregation would be a rector, called by the vestry, instead of a mission vicar, appointed by the bishop and serving at the bishop's pleasure. Trinity's vestry should have been in a joyous mood. Instead of making arrangements for a celebration once the change was approved, Trinity's preparations for council turned into a struggle between the vestry and their vicar. In a meeting prior to the council, the Trinity vestry, by a 5 to 2 vote, ordered its council delegates to "oppose any integration of the races" at Hemlock Haven youth camp "in any way at any time."[194] The vicar, the Rev. John "Jack" Teeter, was outraged by the vestry's action. He charged that the vote was "forced by the segregationist Defenders of State Sovereignty."[195] This group, founded in Virginia shortly after the Supreme Court decision in *Brown v. Board of Education,* was dedicated to strict racial segregation and at its height could boast twenty-eight chapters and 12,000 members throughout the commonwealth. Rather than submit to what he saw as a grave injustice, Teeter resigned his position as vicar. In his letter of resignation, he "opposed both the stance and the heavy-handedness of a vestry that 'would refuse to let a fellow Christian vote as his prayers and conscience direct him to.'"[196] Trinity Rocky Mount would become a parish, but it would do so without a priest.

When the Diocesan Council finally gathered in April, its proceedings provoked a higher than usual interest. Aware of the newsworthiness of the conflict coming out of the last Council this meeting would be closely reported by newspapers such as the *Roanoke Times.* Bishop Marmion tried to set a conciliatory tone in his annual address. He challenged the Council to take "a statesmanlike and forward-looking stand on the racial issue."[197] The bishop urged the delegates to move forward on the summer youth program. "It is imperative," he told them, "that our summer training program for our youth be revived at Hemlock Haven as soon as possible." The bishop went on to plead with the hard-liners to seek some sort of middle ground: "I do feel that if a resolution were offered that did represent a true compromise, with mutual concessions, it might be acceptable to a majority of both orders as a present way out of our stalemate."[198]

Sadly, compromising statesmen were in short supply in Lynchburg that April. Once again, the parliamentary tactic of calling for a vote by orders, where a majority in both lay and clerical ranks was required to pass a resolution, scuttled any hope Bishop Marmion had for an agreement. The first resolution to be considered came from the executive board of the diocese. It asked the Council to approve a resolution that "advocated operating Hemlock Haven on a segregated basis this summer, integrating the conferences for junior youth (below the 10th grade) in 1960, if approved by the 1960 Council, and setting up a racial study commission to seek a solution."[199] This resolution never came up for a vote, as it was buried under substitute motions. Jesse R. Williams, from the predominantly black Church of the Good Shepherd, put forth a complex resolution which, in essence, advocated the total integration of Hemlock Haven.[200] His resolution was voted down by both the clergy and the laity. However, one clergyman lifted a paragraph from Williams's resolution and offered it as an amended resolution: "This Council declares its acceptance with gratitude and its belief in the rightness of the findings of the Fathers in God at Lambeth in 1958; the Anglican Congress of 1954; and the several General Conventions of the Church in the United States in regard to the will of God as to the relation of different races in the Body of Christ; and further, rejoices that it is a part of that One Holy Catholic and Apostolic Church, which has been the means of confronting this diocese with God's Judgment."[201] The Rev. Teeter, recently resigned from Trinity Church in Rocky Mount, rose to support the resolution. Teeter said that "a vote against the resolution would be a 'repudiation' of church doctrine and would mean that 'God's judgement is not applicable in this situation.'"[202]

The lay delegates were having none of it. Gen. E. Walter Opie, the president and publisher of the Staunton *News Leader*, declared, "We shouldn't be put in the position of rejecting doctrine or accepting integration."[203] Robert Whitehead of Nelson County agreed with Opie, stating the matter was one "of policy, not of Christian doctrine." The vote on the amended resolution lost in the lay orders.[204] Once again there was a resolution to integrate Hemlock Haven's summer camp by race but segregate it by sex, the "Perennial Resolution." This time the resolution was proposed by Dr. G. Cary White, professor of sociology at Hollins College. In support of his resolution White stated, "I offer this in the genuine spirit of compromise." The clergy accepted White's compromise by a vote of 37 to 0. However, the lay delegates were unconvinced and rejected it by a vote of 41 to 27. Commenting on the failure of the resolution, delegate Robert Johnson of Wytheville put it bluntly: "The clergy has failed to sell the laymen on integration."[205]

In the end, all had to admit there was no way forward. The Rev. Roger A. Walke, headmaster of Virginia Episcopal School in Lynchburg, addressed the council with this resolution: "Whereas the Diocesan Study Commission has advised the Executive Board that it has not been able to find a solution for the operation of the diocesan youth conferences at Hemlock Haven, which it felt would be acceptable to the majority of both the clergy and the laity; therefore be it resolved that Hemlock Haven be operated in 1959 as it was in 1958."[206] This resolution was passed by voice vote without any division by orders.[207]

The next issue of the official diocesan magazine, the *Southwestern Episcopalian,* attempted to spin as best it could the failure of the 1959 annual council in regard to Hemlock Haven. The May 1959 edition carried the headline, YOUTH CAMP TO BE SHUT AGAIN IN 1959. The opening paragraph of the story was gentle and understated: "The annual Council of the Diocese, meeting in Lynchburg April 16, 17, and 18, calmly handled the problem of the operation of Hemlock Haven by voting that the camp and conference center near Marion be closed to all youth conferences in 1959. The camp will be open for use by parishes and families as it was last year."[208] No mention was made of the wreckage of Bishop Marmion's dreams for compromise or his hope "to find places for convocational and diocesan meetings where there is no discrimination against our Colored brethren." Christ Church vestryman and ardent segregationist Francis West was named in a picture with a group of lay delegates that accompanied the article. The secular press was considerably more blunt about the failure of the council meeting. The *Roanoke Times* ran the headline, "EPISCOPAL CHURCH BARS YOUTH MEETS." The article that followed did not mince words about the final results and which side won: "Passage of the resolution was a victory for the well-organized segregation bound forces of Episcopal laymen..."[209] As a practical matter, the Episcopal Church was racially divided in Southwestern Virginia, and there was no hiding that fact.

18

Maybe the Issue Wasn't Just Race

At Christ Church vestry's May 13 meeting, council delegates Kearfott and West told the members what they by now already knew, "that no (racially) integrated (or de-segregated) youth conferences will be conducted this summer at the summer conference center, Hemlock Haven."[210] As part of this report, it is likely that the vestry heard that once again an attempt was made at Diocesan Council to integrate the youth camp by race but segregate it by gender. Although that proposal had failed, it suggested that there was a subtext to the racial divide—and that subtext was sex.

While in 1959, the delegates in the Diocese of Southwestern Virginia were debating what to do about Hemlock Haven, author Harper Lee was readying a manuscript for her publisher. The following year, 1960, would see the release of Lee's best-selling book, *To Kill a Mockingbird,* a novel centered on a story about the trial of a black man accused of violating a white woman. In that widely acclaimed best-seller, poor white Mayella Ewell receives a beating from her father for kissing black handyman Tom Robinson. To save the family honor, Mayella is forced by her father to accuse Robinson of rape. Despite a brilliant defense to a blatantly false charge, Robinson's attorney, Atticus Finch, cannot save his black defendant from the deep prejudices of an all-white male jury. Southerner Harper Lee was well acquainted with the social mores of Southern society; the code that white men were expected to defend their wives, daughters, and sisters from the purported sexual predations of black males. She would not have been the least surprised that the episode of the Martinsville Seven lingered in the minds of both black and white Virginians—especially in Southwest Virginia—as a cautionary tale.

Just below the surface in the dispute about Hemlock Haven was a sub-context of sexual tension. The "Perennial Resolution" for Hemlock Haven's youth camp—to integrate the campers by race but segregate the camps by gender—had first been proposed in 1958, the same year that interracial couple Mildred and Richard Loving[211] were roused out of their bed in Virginia and arrested for violating that state's miscegenation laws—a marriage that would require the US Supreme Court to decriminalize and validate it. Such tensions over interracial sex caused one religious historian to observe that "the dread of possible sexual contact between black and white teenagers had been a major factor stirring emotions in the Hemlock Haven controversy."[212] The black delegates to diocesan council who vigorously worked for the racial integration of Hemlock Haven felt insulted by the proposals that the racial integration of their children might come only at the price of segregation by gender.[213] In 1961, the newly founded Episcopal Society for Cultural and Racial Unity (ESCRU) held its first meeting in Williamsburg, Virginia, and passed a racially and politically controversial resolution stating that "interracial marriages were not in violation of Christian teaching, natural law, or the Constitution of the United States." In response, the Bishop of West Virginia,

The Right Rev. Wilburn Campbell, accused ESCRU of being an irresponsible organization with ties to the Communist Party. The Rev. Jack Teeter, who attended the ESCRU meeting, called Bishop Campbell's remarks "reminiscent of the era of McCarthyism." At Christ Church, vestryman Francis West immediately called upon Bishop Marmion to disavow ESCRU's approval of interracial marriage. Marmion made no direct response to West's request, although the bishop did comment that he knew of no Communist influence in ESCRU.[214] By 1962, the mixture of sex and race in the Hemlock Haven controversy was openly argued. At the diocesan council that year, Staunton *News Leader* publisher Gen. E. W. Opie declared from the floor of the Council that the opposition to integrated summer youth camps came not from racial antagonism but from fear that mixed conferences could lead to intermarriage later.[215]

Both the church and the government laid claim to determining the operative principles for racial justice in society. There were at least five Episcopalians who were delegates to Diocesan Council and who also served in Virginia's General Assembly. If an important vote on integration was presenting itself at Diocesan Council and the Episcopal members of the Virginia General Assembly found themselves engaged in state business in Richmond, the state legislators would pool their resources to charter a plane to fly to the diocesan meeting and cast their vote for segregation.[216] One of the leaders in both legislative bodies was Virginia Del. Robert Whitehead (D-Nelson, Amherst). Reporting on this convergence of church and state was *Roanoke Times* columnist Melville Carico. In a column he titled, WHITEHEAD AN ENIGMA?, Carico wrote, "In state politics a lot of Mr. Whitehead's thinking went into the concept of 'Freedom of choice' which is now state policy on school integration. And, to advocates of close-the-schools 'massive resistance,' that makes him an integrationist. But, in insisting on 'freedom of choice' within his church, the 62-year-old legislator and lay leader emerged in the image of an unyielding segregationist. Clergymen with whom he and his group differ hold that segregation, at least in church, is contrary to the will of God." Carico went on to explain Whitehead's opposition vote on Hemlock Haven thus: "Mr. Whitehead saw the clergy-backed integration-by-race, segregated-by-sex conferences as depriving parents of 'freedom of choice.' Either they had to send their children to an integrated conference or keep them home."[217]

Few stories capture the confusion of thinking about race as well as Nina Salmon's account of her father, Bishop Frank Vest. As a young priest of liberal persuasion, Vest was seeking to relocate to a church in segregated Virginia. Vest was going through the calling process to become rector of Grace Episcopal Church in Radford, Virginia. One member of the church's search committee said to him, mispronouncing the word, "You know I am not an interracialist." To which Vest replied, "Then why on earth would you want me for your rector?" The man's startling response is typical of the confusion of the times: "Because I would not want the rector of my church to agree with me on that issue."[218]

No one doubted there was a deep divide between many of the lay members of the Diocese of Southwestern Virginia and their clergy. Trippi Penn was still in his teens when his father, Edwin G. Penn Jr., served on the Christ Church vestry during Philip Gresham's rectorship. Penn remembers that Gresham, Bishop Marmion and the clergy of the diocese were in favor of integrating Hemlock Haven, while most of Christ Church's congregation opposed the integration of the youth camp.[219] These differences in Gresham's home parish may have been enough to keep him from delving into diocesan politics. There is no evidence that Gresham was a clergy leader in the diocesan dispute over Hemlock Haven. He never offers a resolution from the floor of council. Unlike lay members of his parish, he is never quoted in the news coverage of council meetings nor is he appointed to any of the committees taking up the matter of integration. However, written evidence and personal memories all agree that Gresham followed his bishop's lead favoring integration. That support did not sit well with many members of Christ Church. As this and other disagreements with the congregation arose, so did insidious speculation about the rector's sexual orientation.

That Gresham almost got married while in Martinsville is a story not widely known. It is a common practice in parishes for members to get to know their priest over dinner at the family's table. Ann Gardner's family hosted Gresham for dinner more than once. Ann revealed that at one such dinner with her mother and stepfather, after receiving a pledge of secrecy, Gresham showed them an engagement ring. Gresham told the members of the family that the next day he was going to Danville, a town about thirty miles from Martinsville, to propose to a woman he'd been seeing there. Ann's impression of the evening was that Gresham was "very much in love." A few weeks later, with no announcement from the church about a wedding for the rector, Ann asked her mother what had happened with Gresham's engagement. Her mother told her that the woman rejected Gresham's proposal and that it had "knocked him for a loop." Ann's mother sternly warned that they were never to speak of it to anyone. The secret of Gresham's failed marriage proposal led the Gardner family to believe that the whispers that their rector might be a homosexual were vicious rumors from people who opposed his stand on racial justice.[220]

In the late 1950s in Virginia, homosexual acts were considered both a sin and a crime. Young unmarried priests, whether gay or straight, were not uncommon in the Episcopal Church and few questioned why a priest was single. On the other hand, gay priests kept themselves deeply closeted, sometimes marrying in an attempt to hide or to suppress their homosexuality. A seminary classmate of Gresham believes Gresham was gay but is of the opinion that Gresham was too much of a gentleman to exercise his sexuality. Such was the common expectation for that generation of priests. The unspoken code was that no one openly spoke about the sexuality of their priest.

Despite what many saw as Gresham's excellent work with the youth group—or perhaps because of it—Charlie Cole remembers that his father never liked Gresham. The fact that the elder Cole was a staunch segregationist was most likely part of the aversion, but Charlie believes it was also jealousy of the friendship that Charlie shared with Gresham. The rivalry the father had with the priest for his son's attention was doubtless real; the youth of Christ Church idolized their rector, and Gresham willingly threw himself into youth ministry. However, some of the activities Gresham hosted for the male youth might have made more than one parent uneasy. For instance,[221] Gresham would invite the members of the high school wrestling club over to the rectory where they would push the furniture out of the way and practice wrestling holds on the living room floor. Today, it is hard to imagine that a bishop would not determine such behavior to be a violation of boundaries by the priest. In the era of the late 1950s and early 1960s, those boundaries could easily have been further called into question by the circumstances surrounding Gresham's relationship with a young man named Sonny Latton.

Gresham met Sonny when Gresham was a curate at St. James Episcopal Church in Richmond and Sonny was living nearby at the youth detention center. The young priest and the troubled youth soon became unlikely friends. Sonny was essentially illiterate, almost a decade younger than Gresham, big and heavyset, where Gresham was short, muscled, and definitely well-educated, but they shared a common interest, wrestling. Near the end of Gresham's first year at Christ Church, Sonny travelled to Martinsville to be with his friend. Gresham gave Latton a room in the rectory and soon afterward signed him up for remedial classes to learn how to read and write. When the members of the wrestling club stopped by the rectory, Gresham and Sonny would demonstrate with each other the proper form for take-downs and escapes. The whole arrangement between Sonny and Gresham was viewed by some as nothing more than a kindly priest living in a large house by himself offering help to a needy young adult who had nowhere else to go. Others suspected that Gresham and Latton were intimately involved, contrary to the laws of church and state. Whatever the truth, as general discord grew throughout the diocese, their relationship only added to the tension in an already stressed congregation.

While largely unspoken, the ghostly presence of sex continued to haunt the racial issue of integration in the diocese. In Martinsville, there arose the added specter of questions about the sexual orientation of the Episcopal priest. The bright spirits of joy and hope from just a few years previous were beginning to dim into fading shadows at Christ Church.

19

"An Unhappy Business That God Has Given"

At the same meeting where council delegates Clarence Kearfott and Francis West informed the vestry that there would be no racially integrated youth camp at Hemlock Haven in 1959, they received a report from Christ Church treasurer Warren J. Watrous that "although no pledge was made by Christ Church in its 1959 budget to 'Builders for Christ' he has been advised by the Diocesan Treasurer that the sum of one hundred dollars ($100.00) has been contributed from Christ Church communicants and Christ Church has been given credit."[222]

Just as small cracks in the foundation often herald larger unseen problems in a structure, the first signs of trouble in a church often come from seemingly insignificant matters. In this case, a group of parishioners donated money to a cause that the vestry had refused to fund. "Builders for Christ" was a program to finance physical improvements to diocesan property, a worthy cause the vestry should have supported had it not included paying the note for Hemlock Haven. It is suspected that the ongoing youth camp controversy was the major influence in the vestry's vote to remove, in a motion made by Francis West, $875 for "Builders for Christ" from the church's 1959 proposed budget. Through this seamless funding barrier, a crack opened large enough to slip in one hundred dollars. Upon the news of this small but unauthorized donation credited to them, the Christ Church vestry acted quickly to seal this gap and reassert its prerogative to control the finances of the church. It voted immediately to "adhere to its adopted budget for 1959 which contained no pledge or allocation" for the "Builders for Christ" diocesan program.[223] Again, in August, the vestry took up the matter of "Builders for Christ" when they instructed Watrous to reply in the negative to a letter from a parishioner inquiring about whether the vestry had altered the budget for that program.

It was not just an unauthorized donation to "Builders for Christ" that annoyed; other small irritants began to strain the corporate nerves of the congregation. Even success was becoming a test of patience. For good or ill, change was exploding at Christ Church in 1959. The growing church membership was overflowing its facilities. In response, the vestry had purchased the Pannill House next door to the church. Such a major acquisition was both exciting and stressful. A church unaccustomed to debt now had to finance the purchase along with the modifications needed for the newly acquired building. This meant a capital campaign to pay for it all. Adding to the stress was the disappointment of finding that the new parish house did not solve all of the church's space problems as quickly as planned. In his report for 1959, Church School Superintendent Bev Parrish wrote, "despite the size of the building, only eleven of our fifteen classes can meet there. Three classes still meet in the basement of the rectory, and one class meets in the Ruth Redd Room." For some in the church, progress was moving too fast, while for others too slow; few escaped the anxiety.

Meanwhile, Gresham's proclivity for high-church ritual rubbed some of his Virginia low churchmen the wrong way.[224] He purchased the church's first processional torches because, as he said, he "loved a parade." When he saw the need, Gresham added a "family service" and changed the time of the other services on Sunday morning, a particularly difficult pill to swallow for the long-term members whose Sunday routine was thereby disrupted.[225] Gresham even had the audacity to request that the vestry allow him to submit changes for the chancel, the most sacred part of the church.[226] The congregation was learning that it had a young, single priest in his first call as the rector of a congregation who had the time, the energy, the ideas, and the authority to make changes to their staid routines. Not surprisingly, Gresham ran into the adversity that is captured in the old church joke, "How many Episcopalians does it take to change a light bulb? Answer: Ten. One to change the bulb and nine to complain about how much better the old bulb was."

Parish House

Any innovation that affects Sunday morning services is difficult for many Episcopalians, regardless of the reason or its benefit. Typically, Christ Church congregation chafed under some of their young rector's breaks with tradition, they disapprovingly pointed to a contrivance the rector used during the season of Lent. In the forty days before Easter, the children and youth of the Episcopal Church had been trained to make daily sacrifices to remind themselves of the sacrifice their Savior, Jesus Christ, made for them on the cross on Cavalry. To this end, the Episcopal Church encouraged its young people to make small financial sacrifices to help the poor and suffering in foreign lands where the Episcopal Church had established missions. The Virginia dioceses customarily supported missions in Central and South America.[227] Each child in Sunday school would receive a "mite box," a small, slotted cardboard container named for the story of the widow whom Jesus commended for putting her mite, two copper coins of small value but all she had, into the Temple treasury. During Lent, children and youth were encouraged to take the pennies, nickels, dimes, and quarters they would have spent on candy, soda, or other treats and put them in their mite box. After Easter, children from throughout the diocese would attend a special ingathering service followed by a celebratory "box supper." The money the children deposited in their mite boxes during Lent would be deposited by the diocese in a mission fund and disbursed to a far-off mission to help the hungry and destitute.

Gresham, always ready to support anything that made Christ Church youth better Christians, designed a clever visual aid to promote the mite box; he strung a wire across the nave of the church from the baptismal font to the pulpit. Hanging from the wire, over the heads of the members in the pews, was a toy "mite box" airplane.[228] As the season of Lent counted down to Easter, Gresham used a stick to propel the toy plane across the church, symbolically bringing relief to the needy children of Central America. Gresham's clever and instructive visual aid for his youngest members was not well received by some of the older ones. Among the adults who loathed any variation within the church's sacred space, the presence of Gresham's mite box airplane during the somber season of Lent verged on the sacrilegious. For these adult traditionalists, the young rector's toy on a wire was just another distraction from the dignity and order that Christ Church had practiced for many years before he arrived.

While the youth program was flourishing under Gresham's guidance, bringing youth to Christ Church from all over the city and from different denominations, some members believed the youth program was adversely taking over the church. Phil Gresham had changed the sleepy Christ Church Youth Group to a dynamo of activity. The rebuff their manifesto received at the annual parish meeting could not "quench the Spirit" in these young people. The Christ Church Youth Group only grew stronger under Gresham's encouraging leadership. The young people of town flocked to Christ Church's undercroft for dances and activities. Other church youth groups would cancel their activities because their teenagers were over at Christ Church.[229] Of course, not all Martinsville parents were thrilled with the idea of their children listening to rock and roll while dancing in the basement of a church on a Sunday night. The Christ Church dances were a big draw for the city's young people, and they were well chaperoned, as Charlie Cole can attest. "Yes, I was caught drinking beer at one of the Sunday night dances in the undercroft," Charlie admits. But such youthful indiscretions were quickly forgiven, at least by their beloved rector. Gresham had a way of seeing the deeper character of the person, which may be why he wrote to Cole a few years later, encouraging Cole to consider going to seminary after college graduation, guidance Cole deeply appreciated but ultimately declined.

Another popular youth activity was the Christ Church coffee house with its beatnik theme. It was in September of 1959 that *The Many Loves of Dobie Gillis* began its four-season run on CBS with Dwayne Hickman playing Dobie, Tuesday Weld as his money-hungry girlfriend Thalia Menninger, and Bob Denver as his way-out beatnik friend, Maynard G. Krebs. The popularity of Denver's character may have inspired the beatnik theme for the coffee house. The gathering was loved by the teenagers but caused perturbed parents to wonder what was going on in the undercroft of their church. The young girls would layer on "eye shadow and mascara to the max" and the young boys dressed all in black, in the Martinsville notion of what New York beatniks might look like. Parents might have saved themselves some worry, as one of the teens who attended tells it, recalling those evenings as basically harmless fun where their teenagers drank coffee, played records on the juke box, and snapped their fingers in approval when the songs ended.[230]

Despite the continued success of many new and innovative programs, a growing group of Christ Church parishioners were learning to dislike their rector and the direction he was taking their church. Gresham's stand on racial integration gave an opening for those looking to undermine his authority. The whispers—it was never more than whispers—about his sexual orientation began. By the beginning of 1960, it became obvious that Gresham's opposition was sitting at the vestry table with him. At the February meeting, the rector gave a list of accomplishments along with his concerns, which mostly grew from the rapid expansion the parish was undergoing. Gresham told the vestry of the "growth in communicant strength; a 30 percent increase having taken place in the last two years." In his eight-point account of achievements were listed the expanded physical facilities, support of seminarians, the addition of a second junior youth group, and what Gresham labeled a "crystallizing of a definite form of Episcopal churchmen." At the conclusion of the rector's presentation, the vestry minutes continue, "Comments from several vestrymen indicated a concern for what might be termed a lack of unity, pointing out that developing and maintaining unification is an important area of work."[231]

It is hard to imagine that the "several vestrymen" unnamed in the February 3, 1960, minutes as being concerned about unity did not include Stafford G. Whittle III, son of the senior warden. Prior to this, after a particularly heated exchange at a vestry meeting, Gresham had excommunicated him.[232] The argument was not recorded in the official minutes, so the exact date of the verbal altercation is not known, but the incident has become part of the folklore of Christ Church. At issue was a dispute over the racial integration of Hemlock Haven. Gresham took the position of his bishop and the clergy of the diocese, that the camp should be open to all regardless of race. The younger Whittle, who was known to have a quick temper, lost his composure and challenged Gresham. He told the priest that he did not care if he was Christ Church's rector, he had no faith in anything that Gresham said or did. When Stafford Whittle finished, Gresham coldly informed him that until he felt differently, he should not come to the altar rail because Gresham would not give him communion, a de facto excommunication. The General Rubrics in the 1928 Book of Common Prayer, the prayerbook in use at Christ Church at the time, permit a priest to refuse Holy Communion to a person who is known "to have done any wrong to his neighbors by word or deed, so that the Congregation be thereby offended"; the priest is further instructed not to administer communion to those in whom he perceives "malice and hatred to reign."[233] Although Stafford Whittle continued to serve on the vestry and attend services on Sunday, he never tested Gresham's resolve by going to the altar rail while Gresham was presiding. For his part, there is no record that Gresham ever followed through on an official excommunication by notifying Bishop Marmion that he was refusing Holy Communion to one of his parishioners, as required by the same rubrics. Regardless of the technical validity of the excommunication, the open conflict between the rector and a member of the vestry, son of the senior warden as well, was not beneficial to harmony in the congregation, to say the least.

Excommunication should always be a disciplinary instrument of last resort, for it removes the communicant from the life of the church community. There is a similar disciplinary instrument reserved for the clergy: Deposition removes the clergyperson from their vocation of sacred ministry to the church community. If the priest is guilty of a gross violation of conduct or belief, the bishop of the diocese can remove the priest from his or her cure and from ordained ministry. For lesser failures, a clergy person can be inhibited, temporarily barred from ordained ministry, often including a satisfactory completion of counseling or rehab. The church has provided canons and procedures for ecclesiastical trials to determine the guilt or innocence of a clergyperson. Such trials are rare. Often, clerical malpractice is resolved satisfactorily with a pastoral "plea bargain" negotiated in the bishop's office with the help of the chancellor of the diocese and all involved parties.

A bit more common is the dissolution of pastoral relationship, the judgment of their bishop that a congregation and a priest sever their relationship. If the calling of a priest can be compared to a marriage between priest and congregation, then dissolution of pastoral relationship is the ecclesiastical equivalent of rector/congregation divorce. Dissolution occurs when the congregation, but most usually, a small, vocal but powerful group within a congregation, dislikes the direction the rector is taking the church or even the manner in which he is taking it. The determined opposition then makes a request for the bishop to intervene in a dispute with its rector, and it is within the bishop's prerogative to declare that the pastoral relationship no longer exists between the priest and the congregation. Before that happens, the bishop is required to seek reconciliation between the rector and the congregation in an unbiased manner. Neutrality can be difficult to maintain for a bishop who knows that it is easier to get another priest than to get another congregation. Too often a weak bishop does what the dissident group in the congregation wants and dissolves the pastoral relationship. Sadly, the dissolution of pastoral relationship is as hurtful, and as destructive, as any messy, contested divorce. It is usually very expensive for a congregation in both lost membership and lost financial support. As with a divorce, hard feelings can last for years. The upheaval it brings has kept the dissolution of pastoral relationship, although more common than it once was, still relatively rare.

Most of the time, the priest and the congregation know when it is time to part ways, and the priest will begin actively seeking a call from another congregation. This knowledge may come by way of overt adverse action by members of the congregation, commonly known as "running the priest off"; some congregations develop a habit of this and earn the reputation as "priest eaters." But most congregations and priests go their separate ways in what could be compared to an uncontested divorce, even a happy parting of the ways. The truth is that in the twenty-first century, pastoral relationships have become more akin to secular career paths than sacred marriages.

For Gresham, the priest that the vestry wanted so badly, the honeymoon period as rector of Christ Church was becoming a distant memory. What had started out as the dream call in

Martinsville began to resemble the words of the Preacher in the book of Ecclesiastes, "An unhappy business that God has given."

20

The Crozier Arrives

After the humiliating dismissal of their manifesto at the annual meeting and the continuing press coverage of their church as a center of hostility to the racial integration policies of their bishop, the importance of Christ Church youth group's peace offering to Bishop Marmion intensified dramatically. Christ Church's youth group doubled down on their efforts to raise money for the bishop's crozier. The fund-raising from dances and the annual Shrove Tuesday pancake suppers continued to be a success. In the summer, they added a "pig picking" as a new way to raise money.[234] The youth group purchased a whole pig and roasted it all night behind the church to be sold as pork plates the next day. Some parents were not thrilled about letting their children stay out all night, but the young people were delighted to play the jukebox and check on the roasting pig until the sun came up. By the fall of 1959, their efforts had paid off and their financial goal was reached for the purchase of the crozier.

The low church history of the Episcopal Church in Virginia meant that this would be the first crozier a bishop of the Diocese of Southwestern Virginia would own. Under the guidance of their rector, the youth group selected a crozier that was simple,

Crozier

elegant, and traditional. Although it was enhanced with silver embellishments suitable to its sacred ceremonial duties, these did not distract from its basic design as a shepherd's crook. It was no surprise to anyone that the high church Phil Gresham was not able to find a suitable crozier from an American church supply house. With money in hand and the exchange rate calculated, the order was placed with a London company specializing in Anglican religious appointments. It was expected that the crozier would not be delivered until the new year, 1960.

Several months went by before the crozier was delivered to Martinsville, early in the new year, as expected. Inside the plain brown delivery box was a hard-sided leather case approximately three feet long, seven inches across and four inches deep. To protect the case and add to its attractiveness, its eight corners had been encased in brass. On one side was a padded leather handle and two locking clasps with keys. The inside of the case was lined in violet velvet. The inside top was padded to protect the crozier and help hold it in place. Imprinted on the velvet lining the lid was a half-inch gold crown with the word *Diadem* emblazoned across it. Three slots in the case held the three round shafts that would be connected by sterling silver joints to make up the crozier shaft's whole length, to be topped with the handsome curved silver crook itself.

After all of their hard work it is easy to imagine the excitement and wonder the young people of the youth group felt as they used those keys for the first time to open the case, then, cautiously, start to unpack and assemble its precious cargo. Perhaps one of the girls who served on the junior altar guild or one of the boys who carried the processional cross cautioned the group about handling polished metal with bare hands. Gloves easily retrieved from the acolyte dressing room would have protected the silver from any marring. It is doubtful that any of them knew the meaning behind the silver maker's tiny hallmarks stamped on each silver piece of the crozier: a walking lion to symbolize that the piece was made in England and a leopard's head symbolizing the City of London. Nor would they have recognized the additional stamps on the top silver pieces: Diadem Sterling of England; B&WL, the stamp of the ecclesiastical silver maker, used from 1924 to 1971 by B&W Limited; and a small cursive letter "d" signifying the year—1959.[235]

When assembled, the three pieces formed a crozier measuring six feet in length. When serving at the altar, the bishop would hold the crozier in his left hand as a symbol of his pastoral office and use his right hand to bless his people. The crozier was magnificent; everything the Youth Group desired for making a peace offering to their bishop. As a final touch, arrangements were made to engrave a brass plaque that would be affixed to the top of the crozier's case. The plaque would read:

The Rt. Rev. William Henry Marmion, D.D.
Third Bishop of Southwestern Virginia
Presented by the Young Churchmen of Christ Church
Martinsville, Virginia
Eastertide A.D. 1960

Brass plaque on crozier case

Sadly, the elation over the gift was extremely short-lived; the crozier had a flaw. To everyone's horror it turned out that the top of the assembled crozier, the crook, had a slight but distinct wobble! Anxious calls were made by Gresham to London to arrange a fix. Gresham described how the crozier as delivered was totally unacceptable as a gift for their bishop. He explained that their plan was to present the crozier to Bishop Marmion at the Acolyte Festival in May. The British company's representative was apologetic and assured Gresham that, of course, they would make any repairs that were necessary, but they could not guarantee that the crozier would be in Virginia in time for a presentation in May. Absent of any workable option, it was agreed by all that the defective crozier would be presented to Bishop Marmion as planned, but, albeit awkwardly, the gift would immediately be retrieved after the presentation for shipping back to London for repair.

21

A Refutation of God's Teachings

While the young people of Christ Church were awaiting the arrival of the long-desired crozier, New Year's Day 1960 had brought with it not only a new decade, but also even more of their rector's dedication of his time and efforts to youth work. The year opened with the Twelfth Night Feast of Lights pageant on Epiphany, January 6. The performance chosen that year was "The Light of the World" by Harold Bassage.[236] Speaking parts went to youth group members John Swezey, Ben Gardner, Newton Colston, Henry Knox-Dick, Kit Swezey, and Mary Cooper Adams, among other participants including the Rev. Gresham. Appropriately, the pageant closed with members of the congregation carrying lighted candles out of the church and back to their homes, symbolizing the light of Christ glowing not only in the church but out in the world and in the home of every Christian. That February, as in years past, Gresham attended the 1960 diocesan Mid-Winter Youth Conference at Natural Bridge, Virginia.[237] During the long winter months at home in Martinsville, the Christ Church youth group was busy constructing picnic tables behind the Parish House for outdoor picnics once the warm weather returned.[238] When Gresham reported in April that he was supervising the work of eight Boy Scouts for their "God and Country" badge, the vestry invited the scouts to appear before them at their next meeting. That May vestry meeting would become one of the most memorable in the long history of Christ Church.

On Wednesday May 4, Christ Church vestry convened their regular monthly meeting in the Ruth Redd Room of the church at 7:30 p.m.[239] The minutes from that meeting show that Phil Gresham presided, as was his role as rector. Present at the meeting were Junior Warden Clarence Kearfott; Finance Committee Chairman Thomas J. Burch; Treasurer Warren J. Watrous; Secretary W. H. Yeaman; and fellow members William C. Cole Jr.; Donald R. Strachan; Charles D. Weaver Jr.; Fred V. Woodson Jr.; Edwin G. Penn Jr.; John Randolph; Roland Rhett; R. M. Simmons Sr.; Stafford G. Whittle III; Frank I. Richardson Jr.; R. M. Simmons Jr.; and Dr. F. Paul Turner Jr. The minutes did not comment about the absence of Senior Warden Justice Kennon C. Whittle. As usual, the meeting began with an invocation from the rector followed by the reading and approval of last meeting's minutes. The vestry then received the report of the treasurer showing the church in a relatively healthy financial position. At this point, the eight Boy Scouts who were working on their "God and Country" awards were brought in to be examined by the vestry. William Richey, Eric Buonassisi, John Buonassisi, James Hill, William Price, Trippi Penn, Ian Knox-Dick, and Joe Kearfott were presented by Gresham, who explained the several phases of their study for the award. The vestry commended the boys for their endeavors and "heartily endorsed" them. Gresham stated that the "God and Country" awards would be presented at Morning Prayer service on May 22, at which time the entire Boy Scout troop would be in attendance for the presentation. After the boys departed, the vestry approved the use of general church funds to purchase the eight scouting awards to be presented. Several other normal business matters came before the vestry and were dispatched in order: repair to the driveway was referred to the Property Committee, a resolution passed authorizing the Property Fund Treasurer to borrow funds to pay on the note for the Pannill house, and a resolution of sympathy was approved for the Jacobs family on the death of Mahlon K. Jacobs.

Next on the agenda was the rector's report. Gresham breezed through four calendar items for the vestry's information: The Laymen's League meeting on May 11; the Annual Diocesan Council meeting on May 12–14, the Virginia Seminary commencement May 24–25 to be attended by Gresham, and the Mite Box Convocation at St. John's Church in Roanoke on May 8. Since Christ Church had a seminarian, J. Thomas Brown, graduating from Virginia Seminary, the vestry fulfilled their canonical obligation to him by reviewing his status and recommending him for Holy Orders. Gresham recommended that the vestry authorize funds for a gift once Brown was ordained. The vestry heard that the rector was planning a vacation to Italy in July and August; the chaplain from Iowa State University, the Rev. Robert L. Walker, would be conducting services while Gresham was away. The minutes do not record any questions or comments on the rector's report. Other bits and pieces of church business from the agenda were considered. The Property Committee presented five bids for painting the rectory; the vestry accepted the low bid. The vestry then approved the purchase of a cover for the choir's piano. At least an hour of very mundane, at times boring, vestry business had been completed when Gresham began a detailed report on youth activity in the parish. He started with an update of a clean-up project in and around the Parish House by the church youth group. Then, he returned to the matter of the Mite Box

Convocation mentioned in the calendar portion of his rector's report. He cited how five days earlier, the Christ Church office sent out a post card to the youth of the parish addressed to their parents. The card was dated April 30, 1960, and read as follows:

> Special Mite Box Presentation Service
>
> On Sunday May 8, there will be a Convocational Mite Box Presentation Service at St. John's, Roanoke, at 4:00 p.m. All members of our church school are urged to attend, and the Canterbury Choir will be vested and in procession.
>
> Please contact the Parish Office during the week if you can help provide transportation, which will leave the church at 2:30 o'clock.
>
> Please remember to bring box suppers. Beverages will be provided.[240]

The church bulletin for Sunday May 1, ran a similar announcement, which was verbally repeated at the announcement time during the service. Referring to these announcements, Gresham informed the vestry that "all of the parishes of the Roanoke Convocation have been invited to this service as well as to the 'box supper' following the service, both being racially integrated."

When Gresham finished his remarks, a "written expression" from Cary J. Randolph addressed to the vestry was presented. Randolph's note read in part:

> While in attendance at the Lay Readers Conference in Roanoke, Virginia, on the past Sunday May 1, 1960, I asked the Rev. B. Clifton Reardon—who bears the title of Diocesan Missioner-Educator—if all churches in the diocese were invited to the Special Mite Box

> Service scheduled at St. John's, Roanoke, for May 8, 1960, and he replied, "Yes." I further asked Mr. Reardon if that included Christ Church and St. Paul's Church, Martinsville, and he replied, "Yes"; and that ended the conversation. When I reached home that same Sunday afternoon, my wife handed me the enclosed card, of particular interest to my two children, Molly and Roberta, both members of our church school. The enclosed card does not indicate that Molly and Roberta are being urged to attend a Negro-White Social.
>
> I do not care to have my children urged to attend anything that the rector of our church must know that I as a Father am deeply opposed to; and I petition you Gentlemen to take such action, if any action be appropriate and proper in the premises, to protect me and all other members of our church from such deception in the future.[241]

The vestry spent some time discussing the note and what action they should take in response to Randolph's concerns. Their judgment was to direct the vestry's secretary "to inform all parents of Christ Church school students and parents of Christ Church Young Churchmen of the fact the Mite Box Convocation and box supper would be conducted on an integrated basis—a fact that had not been previously brought to the attention of the parishioners." The vestry tacitly bought into Cary Randolph's accusation of deception by the rector. It's directing its own secretary to communicate with the parents rather than request that the church office send out the announcement was a not-so-subtle rebuke of the rector and his ability to keep the congregation properly informed. Vestry members, however, were not done admonishing their priest: "The vestry further directed that henceforth announcements and notices of pending meetings must state whether any meeting will be conducted on an integrated basis."

The vestry was taking the extraordinary step of "directing" the rector on how to communicate "announcements and notices" with the people under his pastoral care. Then they went a step further: it would be Gresham's responsibility henceforth, following their guidelines and when the occasion called for it, to stamp some announcements "Not Whites Only." Knowing the extraordinary nature of this directive, Gresham asked that the vote be taken by a show of hands. Two vestrymen refused to vote; the rest raised their hands in the affirmative for adoption of the measure. No names were attached to the votes in the minutes of the meeting.

The vestry meeting continued with reports from Clarence Kearfott on the diocesan Lay Readers Conference and from Stafford Whittle on diocesan meetings preparing for the annual council. A safety measure was passed to fill in the swimming pool that had come with the Parish House. The vestry considered whether they would attend a city Planning Commission meeting that would take up the rezoning of a nearby property. Even as the meeting continued, Gresham was quietly mulling over whether in good conscience he could abide the directives he had just received from his vestry. He gave his answer just as the meeting was about to conclude. When the last agenda item had been reached, Philip Gresham announced that the vestry could expect his formal resignation as rector of Christ Church. He told the vestry that its position on racial segregation was "a refutation of God's teachings and of the policy of the national church." Gresham predicted that, with these views, it would be unlikely that any priest "of the caliber necessary to the continuation and carrying on of the present work of the parish" would accept their call to become rector. Gresham then made his resignation effective immediately, stating that under the circumstances, he could "no longer minister to the needs of Christ Church parishioners." Some members of the vestry attempted to convince Gresham that he should stay through the summer, perhaps hoping that his upcoming vacation in Italy would give him time and distance to change his mind. It is probable that there were a few who cared little whether Gresham stayed or went but were troubled at what a resignation under these circumstances would do to a congregation already struggling with disunity. Gresham's response to pleas to stay was to repeat that his resignation was effective immediately; he was handing over the church and its affairs to the wardens at once.

At this point it is probable that Gresham picked up his effects and walked out of the Ruth Redd Room, leaving the stunned vestry behind to consider their situation. Someone had to notify Senior Warden Whittle about what had just transpired. The last sentence of the May 4 meeting's minutes simply states that, "The vestry deferred action on the resignation until its next meeting."

22

Down by the Hemlock

The morning after the May vestry meeting, the Rev. Philip Gresham rose early, determined to leave Martinsville. He packed a suitcase with the few necessities he would need for a short stay at his mother's house in Richmond. Gresham threw the suitcase in the car, but instead of taking the road to Virginia's capital, he pointed the T-Bird toward Roanoke. Gresham decided he would first make a stop at the diocesan office. The spiritually drained priest felt the need to inform his bishop of what had transpired the previous night at Christ Church and to seek Marmion's guidance. While early May in Virginia was the perfect time of year to drop the top on his Thunderbird convertible, even the fresh air and warm sunshine could not raise Gresham's spirit.

Vestry Secretary W. H. Yeaman also got an early start on Thursday. He needed to record last night's vestry minutes while the events were still fresh. Plus, he had been charged by the vestry to compose a letter for the parents of Christ Church's children. Yeaman began by creating church letterhead on his typewriter:

CHRIST EPISCOPAL CHURCH
Martinsville, Virginia
May 5, 1960

TO THE PARENTS OF CHURCH SCHOOL STUDENTS AND TO THE PARENTS OF YOUNG CHURCHMEN OF CHRIST CHURCH, MARTINSVILLE, VIRGINIA

As has already been announced, a special "mite box" service will be held Sunday afternoon, May 8, 1960, at St. John's, Roanoke, Virginia, to which service all Episcopal church school students throughout the Roanoke Convocation have been invited. Following this service there will be a "box supper" for those who care to remain.

For your information, the vestry of Christ Church herein directs your attention to the possibility that—inasmuch as our convocation is composed of both white and negro parishes—this special service as well as the "box supper" will be on an "integrated" basis.

Very sincerely yours,
CHRIST CHURCH VESTRY
W. H. Yeaman, Secretary[242]

In a small city like Martinsville, the local mail is usually delivered the next day. On Friday, the members of Christ Church would receive Yeaman's letter warning about the integrated Mite Box service and box supper about the same time they picked up their copy of the *Martinsville Bulletin*. On the front page of the local paper, they saw a picture of Philip Gresham above the word, "...Resigns" and a banner that read, "GRESHAM QUITS OVER RACE DISPUTE...Resignation Irrevocable."[243] The article stated that the resignation was the result of a "stormy vestry session" with Gresham resigning because of the "attitude of his vestry toward a racially-integrated children's service." Bishop Marmion was contacted for the article and expressed his sadness over the incident but called the resignation "irrevocable." Speaking about the Mite Box Convocation the bishop stated, "They are not new. They have been held over a long period of time, although not in recent years. It is policy that there be no discrimination in convocation meetings and services of any kind."

Marmion continued, "The Martinsville vestry should have known this, but for some reason it criticized its rector for not calling the attention of his people to it and notifying them of this service." When Gresham was contacted at the home of his mother in Richmond, he gave no other comment than that he would return to Martinsville in the next week to move his personal effects from church property.

On May 11, one week after resigning as rector of Christ Church, the Rev. Philip Gresham wrote two brief notes from his mother's home in Richmond, one to Bishop Marmion and the other to the Christ Church vestry. To Marmion, Gresham typed on his personal Christ Church stationery, "My dear Bishop: This will be the first time I have put the matter in writing, and I feel it is necessary. As of Wednesday night, May 4, 1960, I have dissolved my relationship with Christ Church, Martinsville, and have resigned as rector. From my meeting with you on Thursday morning I am sure you understand the reasons I have taken this step."[244] His note to the vestry was an even briefer two sentences, his formal resignation letter mailed to Yeaman as secretary of the vestry, which they would not receive until May 13. Gresham wrote: "Effective May 5, 1960, I hereby resign as rector of Christ Church, Martinsville. I leave many dear and close friends here, and I pray God's guidance upon the people of the parish."[245]

In Martinsville on that same Wednesday May 11, after the Laymen's League supper, Senior Warden Kennon Whittle presided over a special meeting of the vestry to take action on the verbal resignation of the church's rector. The vestry approved the following letter to be mailed to the congregation on May 13:

> To the Communicants of Christ Church, Martinsville, Virginia
>
> Our dear people:
>
> At the request of the vestry, your wardens direct this message to you with the hope of resolving certain differences of opinion and convictions which apparently exist among some of us, with the hopes of understanding and tolerating our differences in Christian love. Unless we keep the lines of communication open to one another, understanding and unity will be impossible. Certainly it is the vestry's earnest desire to listen to each communicant and to perform its duties in the best interest of all.
>
> Our specific aim herein, then, is to inform you as best we can of actual facts relating to recent events within the life of our parish and to tell you of plans, pursuant to our responsibilities, for carrying on the work of our parish. We feel that debate on these recent events will accomplish nothing but rather may lead to further division, consequently we urge each of you to try and forget that which is past—except to profit by our experiences—and to proceed with singleness of Christian purpose with the work at hand.
>
> We believe that we all deeply regret recent misunderstandings and, especially, the aggravation of these misunderstandings by some incorrect press reports. Even members of our vestry do not always see "eye-to-eye," but every member of the vestry present

at the May 4 meeting—during which the Mite Box Convocation and its "social hour" were discussed, and during which the Rev. Mr. Gresham (not as a aftermath of the discussion) verbally submitted his resignation as rector of Christ Church—can and will state in all truthfulness, that, instead of the meeting being a "stormy" one, the meeting was exactly the opposite. We attribute the description used by some members of the press to the zeal of some reporter or reporters entirely separated from our local scene and entirely unfamiliar with what actually took place. We beg to correct a statement issued by the Bishop—believing that he would want it corrected—stating in effect that the vestry criticized the Rev. Mr. Gresham for not calling to the attention of our people certain aspects of the Mite Box Convocational Meeting. We are not aware of any directed criticism, although, in retrospect, the Rev. Mr. Gresham might have felt that there was. We do feel, however, in view of other events of the past on which there was an understanding between the rector and the vestry, the circumspect procedure for the rector in this case—and in other cases should they have arisen—was by simple announcement to have informed the congregation of these aspects. The vestry's reaction to this omission resulted in the notice recently forwarded to the parents of children and young people in the parish.

The vestry had and holds no intention of attempting to control the attendance or non-attendance of parishioners to group meetings within the diocese.

The vestry and many of our communicants—with no less than the kindest regards and Christian concern for our Negro brethren—have deplored the entrance by our diocese into what some consider to be a sociological problem, a problem so serious and politically explosive as to warrant the best Christian thoughts without agitation and aggravation by the church itself.

We do not subscribe to the theory that good must come as a result of crises. In our own parish there may exist some misunderstandings, even within families. We believe that much might have been done to ameliorate some of these conditions.

Some members of our congregation feel they should be given an explanation as to why the Rev. Mr. Gresham resigned. We do not have that explanation, and, frankly, we were taken completely by surprise by the resignation. Some members may feel that the resignation came because of the lack of cooperation from the vestry. The vestry has never failed to cooperate with the Rev. Mr. Gresham unless its unwillingness to be stifled in certain areas of expression or its failure to be understood can be interpreted as a failure to cooperate. The fact that we sin, both individually and corporately, is readily admitted, but the sin of which some have been adjudged guilty—viz., in the interpretation of Mr. Gresham, a refutation of God's teachings and the policy of the church—is not conceded.

In resigning, the Rev. Mr. Gresham requested that the vestry take no action on his resignation in order that the vestry be not held to blame for it. To have acceded to his suggestion would have placed us in a technical quandary; nevertheless, the vestry did postpone action on the resignation until its next meeting which was held May 11, 1960. Meanwhile, at the meeting in which Mr. Gresham resigned, the vestry left available to Mr. Gresham every opportunity of delaying the effective date of his resignation until after his six-weeks of summer vacation in Rome which he informed the vestry he intended to take. Mr. Gresham was firm in his expressed desire to make his resignation effective immediately. From his remarks in informing the vestry of his resignation, Mr. Gresham's action was not a spontaneous one but one preceded by deliberate consideration and one culminating in his conviction that no longer could he effectively minister to the people of Christ Church.

On May 11, 1960, immediately following the Laymen's League supper and program, and pursuant to due notice to its members, the vestry met and accepted Mr. Gresham's resignation. The vestry unanimously voted to pay Mr. Gresham his salary and car allowance for the entire month of May as well as to leave to his retirement fund credit our parish contribution to the church pension fund for the months of May and June. The vestry asked that Mrs. Ann Krieger continue on with her duties as Parish Secretary and that the church school activities and the church services be continued, for which arrangements have already been made. The vestry appointed a "Call Committee" (composed of Mr. Clarence P. Kearfott, Chairman, William C. Cole Jr., T. F. Gilliam, R. M. Simmons Jr., and Donald R. Strachan) to seek and recommend a new rector for the parish as soon as possible. This committee is already earnestly at work. We know that we have our Bishop's assistance and cooperation in this task. Suggestions from any communicant as to an available replacement will be deeply appreciated.

We do not for one moment desire or expect to call a man who will identify himself with one group to the alienation of another group. We will expect of the rector we call that he act with charity and mature understanding to and for all.

Christ Church has been in existence for practically one hundred years, and some members of the congregation, including the Senior Warden, have been members thereof for more than half a century. We have never before been faced with dissension in the church, and we assure the congregation that such as presently exists (in its limited way) is not entirely due to the fault of the vestry.

With mutual forbearance, faith, and charity existing among us we may look forward—individually and collectively—to progress in the work of Christ's Kingdom.

Faithfully Yours,

Kennon C. Whittle, Senior Warden

Clarence P. Kearfott, Junior Warden[246]

At the end of the letter, it was noted that copies were sent to Bishop Marmion at the Diocesan office as well as to Philip Gresham at his mother's home in Richmond.

The following week, as he had stated to the newspaper reporter, Gresham returned to Martinsville and began to pack his belongings into the Thunderbird. The members of the youth group stopped by the rectory to say their goodbyes to the man who had been their priest, their coach, their teacher, their counselor, their rector, but most importantly, their friend. The youth of Christ Church were devastated that Gresham was leaving.[247] It was as if there had been a death in the parish. Gresham had taken a stand for his belief that racial segregation was unjust and unChristian. Both their priest and their bishop had instructed the Christ Church youth in their Christian duty to love their neighbor as themselves. They stood with their priest and their bishop in opposing the racial separation that their vestry was fighting to keep in place. The Mite Box controversy was simply a continuation of the struggle that first erupted when Marmion proposed integrating the youth camp at Hemlock Haven. Christ Church's vestry led the fight against that proposal and now the youth's beloved rector was paying the price for opposing Christ Church's lay leaders. As Gresham gathered the final cartons into the Thunderbird, eyes began to fill with tears. Ever the good pastor, Gresham let them know that they would be all right and that he would be the same. "Listen," he told the teenagers gathered around him, "I'm in good company. Both Socrates and I went down by the Hemlock!"[248] Despite their tears, no one could contain their laughter as the priest smiled and shook his head. There was a quick series of handshakes and hugs. Then Gresham got into his car and drove toward Richmond.

On July 2, 1960, a thousand miles from Martinsville, the *Milwaukee Sentinel,* in its religion section, carried a brief news item. The article was poorly researched as to time and place, but it got the main elements correct, "DISPUTE: A dispute over segregation prompted the resignation last month of the Rev. Philip Gresham rector of Christ Episcopal Church Roanoke, Va. Gresham favors racially integrated church functions. A number of his vestrymen have been opposed."[249]

23

The Peace Offering

Attendance was not taken at the Mite Box Service or the box supper that followed the service on May 8, 1960, so we do not know who made the trip from Christ Episcopal Church in Martinsville to St. John's Church in Roanoke. Ironically, we do not know if there were any African-American children in attendance at the service or the box supper. After all, there were fewer than 200 African-American communicants in the entire diocese of about 10,000.[250]

The following week saw the forty-first Annual Diocesan Council at R. E. Lee Memorial Church in Lexington. The summer youth program at Hemlock Haven again became the main order of business during the three-day meeting, May 12–14. Fifteen resolutions, amendments, and substitute motions were taken up for the youth program. "It appeared from most ballots that the clergy majority and the minority of the lay delegates amounted to a clear cut majority," the *Southwestern Episcopalian* reported, but as in previous years, the lay delegates called for a vote by orders, requiring both the lay and the clerical orders to have a majority in each house before a measure would be approved.[251] The divided Council was not in an approving frame of mind. Among the measures considered were: a motion to open programs at Hemlock Haven to all young people, which was defeated; a motion that experimental integrated conferences be set up for junior and middle groups of young people segregated by sex, defeated; a motion that experimental integrated conferences be set up for junior boys, defeated; a motion that the entire diocese be polled to determine the future of Hemlock Haven, defeated. On it went with no proposed solution acceptable to the majority of both clergy and lay delegates, including a radical motion from Francis West of Martinsville to get around the issue of integrating the summer youth program at Hemlock Haven by selling Hemlock Haven. His proposal also went down in defeat.

While the seemingly endless debate over Hemlock Haven continued at Council, the newly renamed Episcopal Church Women, also meeting in Lexington, voted 47 to 29 to adopt a resolution urging that the summer camp be opened to all baptized members of the diocese. In this vote, they were joining the diocesan House of Young Churchmen, who had voted three to one at their winter conference at Natural Bridge that they would attend youth conferences held on a non-segregated basis.[252]

With most of the delegates exhausted by the futility of each new vote on Hemlock Haven, the clergy and the lay members of Diocesan Council were forced to concede that they were deadlocked.[253] A motion was made that the summer youth camp be operated in 1960 as it was in 1959 with the exception that college level conferences would be permitted on a non-segregated basis; the motion passed by voice vote of all delegates. However, for die-hard segregationists, even the small exception of racial integration for college students was too big a pill to swallow. During the closing hours of the Council the budget for 1961 was put in jeopardy when the lay delegates proposed a substitute budget that removed the $5,074 portion of the Christian Education fund needed for operation and maintenance of Hemlock Haven. When the Finance Committee refused to accept this substitute budget and reintroduced the original budget that included money to run Hemlock Haven, the lay delegates refused the entire budget. Unwilling to adjourn without a budget for next year, Bishop Marmion declared a five-minute recess to meet with the clergy. When the Council was gaveled back to order, the funds necessary to run Hemlock Haven had been removed from the 1961 budget; this budget passed by voice vote and the Council members, divided as ever, made their way home.

The next week, St. John's Church hosted the Acolyte Festival for the Roanoke Convocation. Recent high school graduate John Swezey, an acolyte and the president of the Christ Church youth group, transported the crozier, still with a wobble, to the festival. It was Rogation Sunday, May 22, and Bishop Marmion had a busy morning preaching and confirming thirty-five persons at St. John's 9:30 a.m. service. At 4:00 p.m., the Convocation's acolytes, dressed in their altar server's vestments, processed into the church to hear an address from their bishop. When Marmion was done speaking, Swezey made his way to the front of the church and, surrounded by his fellow acolytes, handed the crozier, with its elegant sterling silver adornments, to the bishop on behalf of the Christ Church youth group.

It must have been a bittersweet moment for the youths and the bishop. The crozier is a traditional symbol of the bishop's authority and pastoral care. For the Christ Church acolytes there was a profound feeling of loss because their pastor, who had almost certainly conceived the idea for this gift, was absent for the presentation. For the bishop whose diocesan flock had just lived through another divisive Annual Council, the crozier must have felt more like a crutch for support than a symbol of leadership. The gift from the youth group of Christ Church

Martinsville had started out as a light-hearted token of their rector's high church leanings. Over the three years it took to raise the money for the crozier, it had become a profound token of peace and solidarity to a beleaguered bishop from a troubled parish, or at least from that troubled parish's young people.

Immediately after the Acolyte Festival ended, John Swezey approached Bishop Marmion and asked if he could have the crozier back. "It's the wobble," Swezey explained. "We have to send it back to get it fixed." After securing a promise for its return and feigning pained reluctance, Marmion gave up his crozier, the first ever owned by a bishop of the Episcopal Diocese of Southwestern Virginia. Swezey disassembled the pastoral staff and carefully placed each piece in its case for the return to England.

John Swezey was at college for the fall semester by the time the crozier was returned from repairs in London. It fell to the new president of Christ Church Youth, Sue Wooldridge, to ensure that her group's peace offering made it back into Bishop Marmion's hands. Despite the best efforts of the English craftsmen to fix it, the wobble in the crozier never fully went away. Those with a poetic frame of mind muse that the Holy Spirit intended the wobble in the crozier to be a token of how the issue of racial integration of Hemlock Haven shook the Diocese of Southwest Virginia to its core.

24

“My Heart is Still There”

Within a week of Philip Gresham’s resignation as Christ Church’s rector, Bishop Marmion began receiving inquiries from other bishops about the prospects of Gresham considering a call to a church in their dioceses. Marmion was open and honest with his brother bishops about Gresham and the situation that led to his resignation. In a letter to the Right Reverend Anson Stokes Jr., Episcopal Bishop of the Diocese of Massachusetts, Marmion praised Gresham as “a very able young man,” and then acknowledged, “It may be that an older, more mature, person might have handled the situation better, but I am not sure.” He called the situation in Martinsville “very tense…for at least two years.” It was obvious in the letter that Marmion had a real affection for Gresham. “Even the best men on the firing line,” he wrote, “can take only so much before they need a rest or a change of location.”[254]

On June 1, Gresham wrote to Marmion to assure him that, although he had departed the Diocese of Southwestern Virginia, he had not abandoned the priesthood.[255] Gresham shared with his bishop the good news that he received “loads of calls” from churches searching for a priest and that he found two offers “most attractive.” One offer was on the staff of All

Saints Church in Atlanta that included a position as chaplain at Georgia Tech. The other was a call to become the director of religious education for the Diocese of Bethlehem in Pennsylvania. Despite the tantalizing offers, Gresham admitted to his bishop that he was "groggy and confused" from all that had happened. Early in his letter, Gresham allowed the depth of his depression to show, "Let me say right away that my present nether world of opportunity and indecision is a large, fat consummate hell." As a dutiful priest, Gresham knew that he should turn all that troubled him over to God; he admitted he was finding this difficult, "In fact, I'm having a hard time at prayer since I left my parish," he confessed. Gresham confided to his bishop that he thought it was best "not to come to any decision right now at all." Instead, he would go ahead with his planned trip to Rome. Gresham hoped that the three months that he would be away would give him time to figure out what was right for his future and to heal from his departure from Christ Church. "Maybe the fact of the matter is," he told Marmion, "that I just can't get that wonderful parish in Martinsville, and those dear, grand people out of my heart right now. I miss them so very much." Later, in a private letter about Gresham, Marmion would remark to a colleague that Gresham's choice not to jump into a new position was "wisely decided."[256]

All through 1960, Bishop Marmion continued to answer inquiries concerning the availability of Phil Gresham. In response to a letter from Rome as to whether Gresham was qualified as a priest in good standing to receive scholarship help for scholar-priests studying in Europe, Marmion replied that Gresham indeed was a priest in good standing with his bishop's permission to leave the diocese. He went on to recommend Gresham as "one of our fine young clergyman of scholarly aptitude and attainments who should do well in any study program he undertook." Another request for information came from the headmaster of the Brent School in Baguio, Philippines, as to whether Gresham would make a good teacher and chaplain. Marmion replied that Gresham "has the reputation of being creative in his approach to young people though not much of a disciplinarian." Still, Marmion was "glad to recommend" Gresham and stated that "I would not hesitate to consider him."[257]

Gresham took his trip to the Eternal City as planned. His time in Rome was uneventful except for a curious incident that took place in the late summer, the details of which are sketchy and only hinted at in correspondence between Gresham and Marmion. Bishop Marmion became involved in the episode when he received a letter from Europe written by an unnamed man concerning Gresham. As explained in a letter from Gresham to the bishop, this unnamed man stole a Diocesan Council commemorative note pad, which was kept by the phone in Gresham's Rome apartment. Using the church address on the pad, the man wrote Bishop Marmion a bitter letter from Cannes, France. The reason for the bitterness of the letter was explained by Gresham, "As a result of my being 'burned' by the fellow, the Italian police tossed him out of Italy and told him not to return." Further details of this intriguing affair are lost to us, but it must have made Gresham's Roman summer of 1960 memorable.[258]

After his planned three months in Rome, Gresham did not return home. Instead, he headed to Spain for a brief stay and then traveled to England, where he was accepted as a "Recognized Student" at Christ Church College in Oxford.[259] During his studies, Gresham continued to wrestle with his vocation. He wrote to Marmion from Oxford that he "missed so much the roots and family that are a parish." Again, Gresham confided in his bishop his longing for Christ Church. "I haven't yet decided whether it is 'a' parish I miss, or whether it is definitely 'the' parish in Martinsville. Surely, my heart is still there—and perhaps will be until I begin work again." Gresham closed his letter asking for the prayers of his bishop and his brother clergy: "I haven't been able to offer my own very well since May." Marmion responded with words of encouragement and the promise of prayers for guidance and well-being.[260]

The spring of 1961 saw Gresham back in the United States transitioning into a call at St. John's Cathedral in Denver, Colorado.[261] Although happy to be back in parish ministry, Gresham was distressed that he had fallen into a troubled situation at the cathedral. The bishop of the Diocese of Colorado had an ongoing feud with the dean of the cathedral. It appeared to Gresham that he might become collateral damage to their conflict. The bishop of Colorado would not receive Gresham's Letter Dimissory, a priest's official letter of transfer from one diocese to another, until Gresham had been at the cathedral for at least a year. Until then, Gresham would still be under the ecclesiastical jurisdiction of the bishop of Southwestern Virginia even while serving on the cathedral's staff in Colorado. He was, he thought, "a man without a country." Gresham was greatly relieved when Marmion wrote to him that he was "not upset" about the priest's situation and would "just keep you canonically connected" to the Diocese of Southwestern Virginia.

On Thanksgiving Day, Gresham wrote Marmion that he was "delightfully happy" to be at the cathedral and in the city of Denver. The Colorado bishop had given him a position on the Youth Division and he was leading diocesan conferences. However, despite the improving current situation, his future was uncertain because the dean had just announced that he had accepted a call to a church in Winnetka, Illinois. With his dry sense of humor, Gresham wrote about how he and the other two members of the cathedral's clergy staff, the canons, were taking the news, "And just as the horses, wives, and elephants of the Pharaoh are buried with him, we three Canons shall perhaps soon be even more displaced than I am now." Gresham predicted that he would need Marmion's help either for his Letter Dimissory for Colorado if he was allowed to stay at the cathedral or recommendations for a new call if forced to leave. He concluded his Thanksgiving Day letter, "Still, very much, do I miss and love Martinsville—and SW Virginia." A few days later Marmion's reply came in the mail. The bishop comforted Gresham, "Don't worry about your canonical connection with this diocese."[262] Further, Marmion told him that if things did not work out in Colorado, he would help him find another call, perhaps, if one was available, in the Diocese of Southwestern Virginia.

In late January of 1962, Gresham wrote Bishop Marmion requesting his Letter Dimissory. It was a bittersweet development. The Denver Cathedral was now without a dean, but the bishop of Colorado was willing to accept Gresham's transfer anyway. Gresham wrote that he heaved a big sigh of relief to have this matter settled even with the knowledge that in six months the new dean might ask him to leave. His final comment to Bishop Marmion was that as much as he hated to "have his Southwestern Virginia roots clipped," he was anxious to set down roots in Colorado.[263]

On February 1, 1962, the Rev. Philip Gresham was transferred from the Diocese of Southwestern Virginia to the Diocese of Colorado. In his last letter as his bishop, Marmion voiced his hope that Gresham would return home from time to time at least for a visit.

Over the years, Gresham would return for visits to Martinsville, often accompanied by a male companion, and stay at the homes of his former Christ Church parishioners.[264] Gresham eventually returned to Italy and served as the Anglican chaplain in Taramina, Sicily, in the shadow of the

Mount Etna volcano. In 1974, Gresham suffered a partial stroke and took an early medical retirement after 22 years of active ordained ministry. On January 10, 1985, the Rev. Philip Morton Gresham died in Milan, Italy, at the age of 57; his obituary does not mention the cause of his death.[265] Gresham was remembered in death at a Requiem Eucharist held at Christ Church in Martinsville on January 25, 1985; the pew sheet for the service lists John Swezey as one of the lay readers.

25

“The Arc of the Moral Universe is Long...”

On June 1, 1960, less than a month after Philip Gresham’s resignation as rector, the vestry of Christ Church heard a report of a meeting between their Calling Committee and Bishop Marmion. The vestry was told that it was the bishop’s opinion that, contrary to Gresham’s parting prediction, “Christ Church would have no difficulty in selecting a new rector of high caliber, mature outlook and judgment.”[266] It was also reported that, in reply to a committee member’s question, Bishop Marmion stated that the church’s position on racial integration was a matter of policy, not doctrine. At the conclusion of the Calling Committee report, Senior Warden Kennon Whittle “expressed the hope that the subject of integration would never come up again as an issue and that the vestry and parish would go forward united in its work.”

Two months later, vestryman John Randolph received a suggestion from “a friend of the church” to have the Calling Committee consider the associate rector at Christ Church in Charlotte, North Carolina. In response, the Rev. Jere Bunting was added to the list of prospects. By August, the Calling Committee had met with Bunting, a thirty-three-year-old married priest with four children. Favorably impressed, the committee recommended Bunting to the vestry as their next rector. While the exact process the committee used to screen their candidate is not available, there is evidence that one particular issue played a part in their consideration. In making the recommendation for Bunting, Clarence Kearfott, the chairman of the Calling Committee, wrote that "It is our opinion that at diocesan meetings Mr. Bunting would more than likely vote with his fellow clergymen. However, he is a Virginian through and through and certainly will not attempt to stir up any kind of racial questions."[267] Satisfied that this thoroughly Virginian priest would not challenge them on racial issues, the vestry accepted the recommendation of the Calling Committee. With Bishop Marmion's approval, The Rev. Jere Bunting became rector of Christ Church, Martinsville, on September 11, 1960.

Jere Bunting was well liked by most of the members of Christ Church, not in the least because, as predicted, he was the type not to stir up much of anything. Early in his administration he discussed with the vestry how they saw his relationship with St. Paul's Episcopal Church in Martinsville. The vestry agreed that "he should assist this local Negro mission when possible for him to do so."[268] By November of 1962, Christ Church had grown to the point where Bunting asked the vestry to consider giving him permission to bring in an assistant rector. Bunting pointed out that a new assistant could also be helpful to St. Paul's Church, which had been without a priest-in-charge for several years. This suggestion of help for St. Paul's came with a subtle hint about the price of inaction. Bunting informed the vestry that this lack of a priest at St. Paul's Church was of "great concern" to Bishop Marmion, who "offered the suggestion that the Rev. Mr. Teeter, of Lynchburg, Virginia, might serve St. Paul's."[269] The reaction by the Christ Church vestry to Marmion's suggestion of a priest for St. Paul's Church was swift and strong. The vestry minutes state, "They unanimously expressed opposition to the suggestion regarding Mr. Teeter."

The vestry knew the Rev. Jack Teeter by reputation, a reputation that was not held in high esteem by them. After Teeter's 1959 resignation from Trinity Episcopal Church in Rocky Mount, protesting the vestry's decision to require its delegates to oppose the racial integration of Hemlock Haven, he accepted the call as vicar of the predominantly African-American Lynchburg parish, the Chapel of the Good Shepherd. While there, Teeter became deeply involved in racial justice issues in Lynchburg. On December 14, 1960, at the segregated lunch counter of Patterson's Drug Store in downtown Lynchburg, six college students, four white and two African-American, were arrested and charged with trespass when they staged a peaceful sit-in.[270] As vicar of The Chapel of the Good Shepherd and as a member of the NAACP, Teeter felt a duty to support the "Patterson Six" when they came to trial.[271] The Episcopal priest's support did not go unnoticed. Roanoke station WSLS TV broadcast news footage of Teeter and others entering the courthouse.[272] The *Roanoke Times* reported that during the hearing, Teeter "was forcibly ejected from the courtroom when he attempted to sit in the section reserved for Negro spectators." The priest being unceremoniously removed from the court by uniformed police was captured on film. Claiming that his civil rights were violated, Teeter complained to the Justice Department in Washington, but nothing came of it.[273] As for the "Patterson Six," they were sentenced to 30 days in jail.

Jere Bunting waited until the end of the 1962 December vestry meeting to drop a bombshell on the members. As Bunting had forewarned them at the previous meeting, Bishop

Marmion had assigned the Rev. John Teeter to St. Paul's Church in Martinsville effective December 16 "and for an indefinite period."[274] Teeter would continue to reside in Lynchburg but would conduct services every Sunday evening at St. Paul's Church and "devote Mondays to ministering to its communicants." Furious with Marmion's decision, "the vestry discussed the bishop's action in this matter at length." Three days later a special meeting of the vestry was called for the sole purpose of discussing "the recent action of the diocesan bishop, The Rt. Rev. William H. Marmion, in assigning the Rev. John (Jack) Teeter to St. Paul's Mission in Martinsville, contrary—although the bishop's prerogative—to the expressed wishes of Christ Church vestry as recorded in its minutes of November 14, 1962."[275] It is obvious that the vestry of Christ Episcopal Church was overly impressed with itself if it thought it had any say in who the bishop could or could not choose to pastor a church in his diocese. The minutes of the special meeting clearly convey both the anger and the anxiety of the Christ Church vestry:

> As expressed by some vestrymen, concurred by all members of the vestry, this action on Bishop Marmion's part—particularly in view of related issues of the past several years—was considered an effrontery; however, through the Rev. Mr. Bunting, Bishop Marmion informed the vestry that his action was not intended as such. The vestry, nevertheless, expressed grave concern over this appointment, especially because of the Rev. Mr. Teeter's past activities in racial problems and disturbances in Lynchburg, Virginia, which have stamped him as a most controversial figure and one who could seriously disturb good race relations presently existing in Martinsville if he chooses, a possibility extending its effects far beyond

> the parish level and to the detriment of the entire community. Generally, except for Bishop Marmion's apparent continued disregard of the vestry's wishes and convictions in this field, the vestry expressed its lack of understanding of both the urgency in assigning a priest to St. Paul's and the 'motivation' behind this particular assignment.[276]

Christ Church vestry was in an ill mood and they wanted Marmion to know it. The vestry unanimously voted to appoint a special committee "to present the vestry's position and concerns" to the Diocesan Executive Board despite the fact that the Executive Board, responsible for the finances and property of the diocese, had no say in who the bishop could appoint, as the vestry had already acknowledged. Christ Church's vestry added gravitas to their special committee with a motion that stated Christ Church would pay their monthly obligations to the diocese. This, of course, was a totally unnecessary motion, though it was a not-so-subtle threat. Marmion and the Executive Board were being warned that there could be financial consequences if the bishop continued to ignore the concerns of the Christ Church vestry.

It was less than four days until the Diocesan Executive Board was scheduled to meet. Not willing for the diocese to be drawn into a public battle with Christ Church, Bishop Marmion requested an immediate conference with the entire vestry. One day before the Diocesan Executive Board meeting, Bishop Marmion made his way to Martinsville. The bishop explained to the vestry that as diocesan bishop he had "as much at stake" in avoiding "explosive situations to the detriment of the church and the community." Marmion laid out the limited options he faced. St. Paul's was "urgently in need of leadership" and his choice was to send Teeter, "his only available priest," or send no one at all. The vestry was not convinced. Francis West along with three other members of the vestry "impressed upon the bishop the seriousness of the situation," calling Marmion's assignment of Teeter to St. Paul's Church "a grave mistake and error in judgment." At the end of the meeting the vestry felt it had received the bishop's assurance that Marmion "would terminate the assignment" after a meeting with the vestry of St. Paul's Church and with Teeter. For their part, Christ Church's vestry voted to rescind its vote to send a special committee to the Diocesan Executive Board.[277]

Two days before Christmas, the Christ Church vestry called its third special meeting in December to express, once again, their anger and frustration with Bishop Marmion. Contrary to what they believed had been promised, the matter of John Teeter and St. Paul's Church was not raised at the Diocesan Executive Board meeting. The vestry "unanimously endorsed and approved" a strongly worded letter for delivery to Bishop Marmion and copied to the Venerable B. Clifton Reardon, archdeacon of the diocese. In the letter, the vestry complained to the bishop that they were "distinctly under the impression... that you were inclined to understand our thinking; that you were sympathetic with our position; and that you would correct that which was agreed upon as being a mistake." Christ Church leadership made it clear to the bishop that Jack Teeter was not to minister in Martinsville. It did not matter to the vestry that their meeting with the bishop was less than four days previous and it was the height of the Christmas season; there was no reason for Marmion to delay informing Teeter that he was not welcome in Martinsville. "We assumed," they wrote, "as a result of our discussion, that you intended to take a strong position in the matter and would retract the Rev. Mr. Teeter's appointment. It was thought, too, that this would be done quickly because of the obvious disadvantages of delay."[278]

On the day after Christmas, Marmion mailed a letter to Christ Church acknowledging the receipt of the vestry's letter of December 23 and informing them that on Christmas Eve he had rescinded the appointment of John Teeter as vicar of St. Paul's Church.[279]

The leadership of Christ Church continued to lock horns with their bishop. The arena for the struggle continued to be the Diocesan Council. At the May 1962 Diocesan Council meeting, the clergy and lay delegates continued their split over the integration of Hemlock Haven. As he did in 1960, Christ Church delegate Francis West again championed the sale of Hemlock Haven rather than its integration. West's picture appeared in the *Roanoke Times* with the caption, "Francis T. West...Wants 'Malignancy' Removed"—a reference to his statement that the council should "...remove a malignancy that is sapping the strength of the diocese."[280] Defeated again was the "Perennial Resolution" to integrate the camp sessions by race but segregate by gender. Also, defeated was the "Double Track Plan" to have one whites-only camp and one racially integrated camp. With the deadlock continuing, the council abruptly adjourned without approving an operating budget. Unable to administer a diocese without a budget, Marmion was forced to call a special council meeting for September. In the interim the Diocesan Executive Board worked on a compromise for Hemlock Haven that they hoped would lead to the approval of a budget. After five years of controversy over Hemlock Haven, both the clergy and the lay delegates agreed to the "Perennial Resolution," a motion made in 1958 by Jack Teeter the first time the summer camp was discussed. Hemlock Haven would have six summer camps, three for boys and three for girls, integrated by race. In a speech at council Francis West stated, "It is painful to the core to effect a policy in contradiction to conviction."[281] Half a decade of controversy over Hemlock Haven had ended.

The end of the struggle did not insure a victory for Hemlock Haven. The diocesan camp and conference center never became the success Marmion had hoped for. In 1985, after years of financial struggle, the Bishop Phillips Memorial Center at Hemlock Haven was sold to the Commonwealth of Virginia.

The controversy over Hemlock Haven was bitter and confusing. It undeniably had racial issues at its core. The "solution" of 1962, integration by race but segregation by gender, showed that there was a definite sexual component to the racial divide. The continuous voting by orders over numerous councils demonstrated that authority in the church was also a concern. At the vestry meeting of February 13, 1963, Christ Church rector Jere Bunting read portions of a letter addressed to Francis West from the Rev. Robert Breeland, assistant rector of All Saints Church in Atlanta, Georgia, but formerly rector of Grace Church, Lynchburg, during the Hemlock Haven controversy. In his letter, Breeland stated to West that he "disagreed and still do" with the position West took on the issues. However, he thanked West for "upholding the authority of the laity in our church," adding that "the give-and-take sharing of authority in our church needed to be preserved and honored" or else "the church would quickly become clerically dominated, and its demise would follow immediately." Breeland's appreciation of West's upholding of lay authority in the church by standing up for segregation closely echoes the argument that a personal loathing of slavery should not keep one from thanking the Confederacy for its defense of states' rights. The gratitude is not deserved in either case.

Michael Muse, who was the first African-American student to break the racial barrier at Martinsville High School, was also among the first black campers at Hemlock Haven. After listening to Muse talk about his experiences at Hemlock Haven, you will never prove to me that the battle to integrate the camp was not worth it. After the compromise worked out in September of 1962 at diocesan council, the summer youth program scheduled separate camps for junior girls (grades 4, 5, 6), middle girls (grades 7, 8), senior girls (grades 9, 10, 11, 12) and camps for junior boys, middle boys and senior boys, all integrated by race. By 1967, the racially integrated senior camp included both boys and girls. In 1969, the racially integrated coed camps expanded to include a senior camp (grades 10, 11, 12) and a junior high camp (grades 8, 9). Some separation by gender continued into the '70s but, at least by 1977, all camps were integrated by race and gender.

Michael Muse loved that camp. Muse was a member of St. Paul's Episcopal Church in Martinsville, less than a mile from Christ Church, but he will tell you that it was at Hemlock Haven that he had his first encounter with white Episcopalians. He made friends at Hemlock Haven, black and white, male and female. He referred to one female camper from Roanoke as a "best friend," although, even fifty years later, he would not divulge her name to me. The black and white campers ate at racially integrated tables and slept in racially integrated cabins. Bishop Marmion's dream of racial harmony in his diocese was on display with the children at Hemlock Haven.

When Muse returned from camp to Martinsville, he started to identify Episcopalians at his high school. Friendships developed and deepened. Muse was delighted but not surprised when, after a big high school junior-senior dance, he was invited to an after-party at Christ Church by Episcopalian classmates. So it came as a deep and painful shock when he and his date were refused entrance to the party at the church door by Christ Church's priest. When I queried Muse about the name of the priest who blocked his entrance, he was unsure, but the episode left such a deep scar that Muse left the Episcopal Church for several years.

I found it painful to listen to the story of such a humiliating rejection of an African-American Episcopal youth by an Episcopal priest. There simply was no excuse for such behavior, but perhaps I could discover a reason, even a poor and misguided one. I learned that during this period the Diocese of Southwestern Virginia was closing some of its smaller, poorer churches and combining their congregations with larger, wealthier churches. Bishop Marmion hoped that this strategy would result in larger, stronger, and, importantly, racially integrated congregations, because, not surprisingly, many of the churches that were closed were the poorer, smaller African-American churches. Despite Marmion's good intentions, the Episcopal African-American community grew resentful that it was their churches that were being closed and their congregations that were being asked to blend into the larger, white congregations. There is not an instrument to measure the level of welcoming that the white Episcopal congregations extended to their new black members. Anecdotal evidence seems to indicate that the degree of welcome was inconsistent throughout the diocese. Half a century later, Martinsville has the distinction of having the last of the historic black Episcopal churches in the Diocese of Southwestern Virginia. I have always preferred to believe that St. Paul's Episcopal Church's survival was the triumph of its congregation's tenacious resolve to retain its proud heritage rather than Christ Church's lack of welcoming. During my research for this book, when I mentioned that a priest turned away a black Episcopal youth from a youth event at the church, it was explained to me that the priest was probably just doing what the vestry told him to do. It might indeed have been the reason, though an inexcusable one.

Justice Kennon Caithness Whittle died on November 10, 1967, at the age of seventy-six after a long illness following a stroke.[282] Befitting his esteemed place in the community,

Whittle's obituary and picture ran on the front page of the *Martinsville Bulletin*. The Rev. Paul Pritchartt, rector, presided at the burial from Christ Episcopal Church where Whittle had served on the vestry, mostly as senior warden, for fourteen years; upon his resignation from the vestry he was elected Senior Warden Emeritus. As a jurist, Judge Whittle had the remarkable distinction of never having had any of his decisions reversed by the Virginia Supreme Court of Appeals.[283] As an Episcopalian, however, Senior Warden Whittle was considerably more fallible. Ultimately, the Diocesan Council rejected Christ Church's position "that the intermingling of the races, in addition to being illegal, can, in our view, only lead to bitterness, discord, and confusion among our people." This reversal of the opinion of Whittle's vestry did not happen as quickly or as amicably as a good Christian would hope, but happen it did. Today, no vestry of the Episcopal Church would ask its rector to accept the proposition "that the segregation-integration question was a political-social question having no connection with religion." Such a position would be contrary to the Baptismal Vows in the Book of Common Prayer that bind every baptized person to "strive for justice and peace among all people, and respect the dignity of every human being." Gone from the Episcopal Church are the overt prejudices of the type found in Whittle's vestrymen, a group of Virginia gentlemen steadfastly devoted to upholding the Southern legacy of white supremacy enshrined in the laws of the Commonwealth; vestrymen who took the position that the church's role was to buttress the political and legal establishment that provided peace and harmony for their class of society. That those ideals lasted as long as they did is still something deeply disturbing, to say the least.

Virginia is fraught with such enigmas. If cognitive dissonance had a home, it could well be somewhere in the Commonwealth. Perhaps it would be somewhere near

Monticello, the home of the slave owner who help found a nation dedicated to the proposition that "all men are created equal." Perhaps it would be near Mount Vernon, where the hero of the War for Independence and the "Father of his Country" kept his slaves. It could even be near Martinsville, where a church would hold nationally recognized seminars that theologian Reinhold Niebuhr called "the greatest expression of religion I have ever seen," yet that same church would lose its priest over a conflict about letting its white children eat a box supper with black children at a church event to benefit hungry brown children.

The stormy departure of Phil Gresham from Christ Episcopal Church in Martinsville was all but inevitable. Even though in *The Living Church* article, he had advised others that priests should not leave their parish over the battle for integration, ultimately, the segregationist position of the church's leadership was more than Gresham could tolerate and so he resigned as rector. With Gresham's departure, Senior Warden Whittle and Junior Warden Kearfott wrote to the Christ Church members "with the hope of resolving certain differences of opinion" and informing them "as best we can of actual facts relating to recent events within the life of our parish" while also admonishing them that "debate on these recent events will accomplish nothing but rather may lead to further division." The wardens laid part of the blame for whatever misunderstanding existed in the congregation about the rector's departure on "some incorrect press reports," a polite way of saying "Fake News." However, there is nothing in the May 4th meeting's minutes that supports the wardens' contention that Gresham's resignation was not the aftermath of the mite box discussion or that "Gresham's action was not a spontaneous one but preceded by deliberate consideration." If the wardens' version of events is true, it is difficult to understand why Gresham didn't have a resignation ready to leave with vestry secretary Yeaman that day rather than taking the a week to write a two sentence resignation that he mailed to the vestry. The wardens went on to state that the reported criticism of Gresham by the vestry never took place. As for the accusation that the vestry did not cooperate with Gresham, the wardens suggested that it was the vestry that was stifled and misunderstood by the rector. The best course forward for the congregation, the wardens suggested, was "to try and forget that which is past—except to profit by our experiences—and to proceed with singleness of Christian purpose with the work at hand." Given this understanding of the events surrounding the prior rector's departure by the wardens, it came as no surprise that Christ Church's vestry would choose as Gresham's successor "a Virginian through and through…[who] certainly will not attempt to stir up any kind of racial questions."[284]

Christ Church vestry was convinced, and attempted to convince their congregation, that when it came to issues of race, they acted in the best interests of the church and in accordance with the laws of the Commonwealth of Virginia. The culture war of racial integration had reached from the schools of Topeka, Kansas, to the youth cabins of Hemlock Haven to the children's dinner tables at diocesan Sunday gatherings. As a justice of the Supreme Court of the Commonwealth and surrounded by politicians and lawyers on the vestry, Senior Warden Whittle knew the law was on his side. With feigned concern, these honorable Christian men insisted that they meant no harm to the African-American population in their midst, but only to maintain peace and tranquility within the law. Although the reins of power were in their hands, they took the posture of the victims in their fight to keep black children from invading their white children's summer camp. Despite their position of power, they operated as clandestine rebels upholding the traditional values of the culture and the historical traditions of their church against the relentless forces of a vast cultural experiment.

If all of this has a familiar ring, it is because though the substance of the argument has changed, the form has been constant throughout history. It is very similar to the arguments made by the priest of King Jeroboam against Amos the Prophet in ancient Israel; to the arguments made by the religious authorities in Jerusalem against Jesus and, later, his disciples; to the arguments made by the secessionist slave owners prior to the American Civil War; to the arguments made by the Gilded Age capitalists against nascent unionists striving to make a living; to the arguments made by paternalistic politicians who opposed the suffragettes; and, most recently, the arguments made by right-leaning Christian Evangelicals against those opposed to their demands to codify traditional family values in a Christian nation. In different places in different eras, the established authority of an oppressor was challenged by the moral force of marginalized instigators. Each time the oppressor sought to discredit their opponent by labeling them as the enemy of law and order and accusing them of subverting the peace of the land. If it was not possible to label them as godless, these instigators were accused, at minimum, of perverting the sacred traditions of religion. What was most astounding is that in the contest between the powerful and the marginalized, it was the powerful who tried to convince the world that they were the victims of an attack by sinister forces destructive to society.

The subterfuge of oppressor posing as victim has been a common ploy throughout history with varying success in winning the common folk to see themselves as victims and in giving them permission to join in the oppression. Success in this instance can reverberate through decades, even centuries until the deceit is exposed. Each new generation, then, owes it to the next generation to reflect on its history; to unflinchingly strive to find the truth of "how it was." Without honest reflection on the thoughts, motivations, and deeds of the past, our present situation will be distorted by vague notions, false justifications, and the pseudo-heroics of imagined history. The centuries are littered with the consequences of refusing to face honestly "how it was"—from the pogroms caused by blaming the Jews for killing Jesus to our own divisive American myth of the "Lost Cause."

A century and a half after Appomattox, we still suffer from a false notion of the cause of the War between the States. Despite contemporary statements that the Confederacy was formed to safeguard the divinely bestowed white privilege of enslaving a naturally inferior black race, many Americans still believe the myth that Southern patriots were defending a noble way of life against Northern aggression hell-bent on dictating changes to a culture they did not share or understand. But the "Lost Cause" is not how it was, ever. It never existed outside of illusory films like *Birth of a Nation,* fanciful books like *Gone with the Wind* and the minds of those facing fading advantage, for whom the sweep of cultural progress is perceived as being brushed aside. The tenacity of the myth of the virtuous rebel fending off aggression is the reason the Confederate battle flag of the Northern Virginia army is still seen at conservative political rallies. The mythological Confederacy has not yet surrendered, but its defeat is inevitable because truth is more powerful than false myth.

Influential and powerful in their time, segregationists are now regarded as having been on the wrong side of history. In their heyday, the proponents of Jim Crow laws would claim that public opinion, centuries-long tradition, political will, contemporary science, and popular religion were all on their side. Yet, the moral arguments for our common humanity in a just society proved more formidable than all of the legal, political, pseudo-scientific, and quasi-religious arguments of the segregationists. The lesson of history is that it is immoral and unjust to deprive a child of a good education because the law says he cannot attend school with children of a different race. It is unthinkable that history will not judge that it is immoral and unjust to forcibly separate children from their parents and put them in cages despite all of the legal, political, pseudo-antiterrorism, and quasi-religious[285] arguments made for the separation and incarceration of children. Condemnation will fall especially hard on those church leaders who misrepresented the Gospel in an attempt to give religious cover for acts of bigotry against poor, brown-skinned families.

26

"...But it Bends Towards Justice"

The vehement resistance to integration within the church is painful to acknowledge for those of us brought up to think of that fellowship as the body of Christ. There is a feeling of despondency among the faithful when the church seems to have difficulty recognizing right from wrong. One of the great contributions of Anglican thought that helps with working through this disappointment is found in the Articles of Religion. There it states that even the great Church Councils "gathered together, (forasmuch as they be an assembly of men, whereof all be not governed with the Spirit and Word of God,) they may err, and sometimes have erred, even in things pertaining unto God."[286] Anglicans are admonished to heed the Apostle Paul's warning that even the saints have to work through their salvation with fear and trembling.[287] The grace for honest reflection forces us to admit that knowledge is often purchased with the currency of past mistakes.

Historians caution that it is a common error to try to understand the past on our terms rather than the terms of the people who lived in the era.[288] The church has long subscribed to the Doctrine of Invincible Ignorance that protects past generations from the arrogance of the judgments deemed modern and enlightened by each new generation. People cannot be blamed for what they cannot know. However, what is unknowable should not be confused with the refusal to accept the reality of what is knowable because it is adverse to my identity, uncomfortable to my position, or currently unpopular in my society. Most people recognize that ignorance is not a virtue and that there is an expectation that we should at least try to be smarter; try to be better. Jesus promised his disciples, "You shall know the truth and the truth shall make you free."[289]

If the church is not infallible, at least the faithful can assume that in its two millennia the church has amassed a treasury of moral certitude that it dispenses to help make the world a better place. As reassuring as this guidance may be to the average Christian, the primacy of the church's moral instruction is accepted in theory more readily than in practice. Most clergy know the sermon illustration about the preacher who tells his congregation to be like the New Testament good Samaritan and to lovingly care for those who are different from them—then goes on to tell them that it is immoral for their country club to exclude minorities and that they should right this wrong. After the service the preacher is informed in no uncertain terms by his irate listeners that the sermon strayed from preaching and wandered into meddling. Every congregation has unspoken lines drawn between preaching and meddling on topics as many and varied as the people who fill the pews.

I let myself get disappointed when the topic of race comes up at church because some church members continue to regard racial issues as a social problem tangential to the moral teachings of the church. Although I know that my beloved Christian church was home to both moral gallantry and collective timidity amid the racial strife of the civil rights era of the 1950s and '60s, I feel dispirited when I see the avoidance exhibited by some of my fellow Christians in the struggles surrounding race and culture today. The ability to honestly face "how it was" is a gift for those who are willing to reflect on the past in order to understand the present. And I, like everyone else, needs to remember "how it was" and then to rejoice that "it" is still evolving.

As we have seen, there were strong feelings that the struggle for integration and racial equality was a "sociological problem" that should never have become an "unfortunate controversy" for the church. The advice was given that this matter should be forgotten by the membership so that the work of the church could move forward. The Gospel tells us that Jesus' ministry came under suspicion from the religious leaders of Jerusalem because, unlike John the Baptist, Jesus did not live a life of solitary austerity, eating locusts and wild honey while living alone in the desert. Jesus was accused of being a glutton and a drunkard seen in the company of prostitutes, tax collectors, and sinners. How could Jesus teach people to be holy, his critics chided, if he became involved in the problems of the world? Rather than argue with his detractors, Jesus replied, "Wisdom is justified by her children."

In Christ Church, Martinsville, it was the youth of the church who followed our Lord's command to "Love one another" even when others around them were being unloving. For this they had the guidance of a reluctant hero in the person of the Rev. Philip M Gresham. He bent over backwards to try to understand his congregation and to keep peace among his lay leadership. Did he bend too far? The 21st century reader finds Gresham's defense of his vestry that "Some mighty fine Christians are segregationist" especially cringeworthy. However, when he was forced further than his conscience would allow, Gresham snapped back, took hold of his principles, and paid the consequences for it. As one who sat in Gresham's chair as rector, I find it is hard not to feel sorry for Phil and yet, to envy him at the same time. Gresham was thrown into a situation that would have challenged any older, more seasoned priest. He found himself opposing people he truly loved and admired. It is open to discussion whether he ever recovered from being rector of Christ Church, and that is sad. Still, who could not envy being "the greatest priest ever" in someone's life? Gresham was that to more than a few of his youth group. I know the adults that they became, and they are Gresham's crown and his glory. I envy him that; anyone would.

Greatness is often born out of adversity. The dispute over Hemlock Haven challenged the church to engage with an injustice that it had avoided for too long. Finally, in imitation of their Lord, church leaders like William Marmion and Philip Gresham plunged into the racial fray to show there was hope for the church and to call the world to repentance. Despite warnings from its lay leaders that this was a social not a religious matter, the church promised, as did its Lord, that its deeds on behalf of the oppressed, its children, would prove it right.

Often moral proof takes decades to be realized. Martin Luther King Jr. confidently predicted, "The Arc of the Moral Universe is long, but it bends towards Justice." The story of the hard-fought integration of Hemlock Haven provides an example of repentance, forgiveness, and a promise that how it was is not how it has to be...as we all learned at the 1993 Diocesan Council of the Diocese of Southwestern Virginia.

Bishop Marmion retired in 1979, just as controversies over women's ordination and the introduction of a new Book of Common Prayer were heating up in the church. Commenting on Bishop Marmion's retirement, the Presiding Bishop of the Episcopal Church, The Most Reverend John Hines, said of Bishop Marmion, "His Christian charity outlived his severest critics."[290] He was succeeded by The Rt. Rev. A. Heath Light. Marmion was present at the Diocesan Council of 1993 when it was announced by the Stewardship Committee that an endowment of $75,000 in honor of him was being established by Francis T. West to fund the Bishop Marmion Resource Center; the announcement being made "at this time for two reasons: first, so that Bishop and Mrs. Marmion can be aware of the honor during their lifetimes, and second, in the hope that others may be inspired to make similar gifts."[291] Since Francis West was out of town on business, his son Frank West, delegate from St. John's Church in Bedford, addressed the assembly on his father's behalf. Through his son, Francis West admitted that he and Bishop Marmion had had many differences years ago, but that they continued to respect each other in spite of differences. Frank West continued speaking for his father and said, "The bishop not only presided over Council, with grace, dignity, and absolute fairness, but exhibited the same courtesy to me when he came to my parish and my home. Both of us held strong but differing views, but I have long since come to the realization that there was more right on his side than mine."[292] Only a few persons in the room understood the full meaning and the power of grace that created this moment. Christ Church delegate Sue Wooldridge Rosser, youth group member from the Gresham years, was one of these. All of the delegates at Christ Church's table fought back tears. When Frank West finished reading his father's letter, Bishop Marmion came forward and spoke, "Thirty years ago I would have said, this is a miracle. Today I am convinced that it is the work of the Holy Spirit which has brought healing to our diocese."

The Right Reverend William Henry Marmion died in a Roanoke, Virginia, nursing home on May 30, 2002, at the age of 94.[293] He outlived his brother and fellow bishop, Gresham Marmion, by two years and his wife, Mabel, by only six months.

Francis T. West died November 24, 2007, in Roanoke, Virginia, at the age of 87.[294] He was buried from St. John's Episcopal Church in Roanoke where the diocesan council had hotly debated Hemlock Haven. The family asked that in lieu of flowers, contributions be made to Christ Episcopal Church, Martinsville.

In 1986, a brushed metal memorial plaque was conceived, paid for, and presented for dedication at Christ Church by members of Phil Gresham's youth groups; it hangs in the church's narthex. It reads:

To The Glory Of God
And In Loving Memory Of
The Reverend Philip Gresham
1927 ~ 1985
Rector Of Christ Church
1956 ~ 1960
Inspired Preacher
Lover Of Worship
Teacher Of Youth
Bold Prophet

"The peace of god, it is no peace,
But strife closed in the sod.
Yet, brethren, pray for but one thing -
The marvelous peace of God."

Given by the members of his youth groups
1986

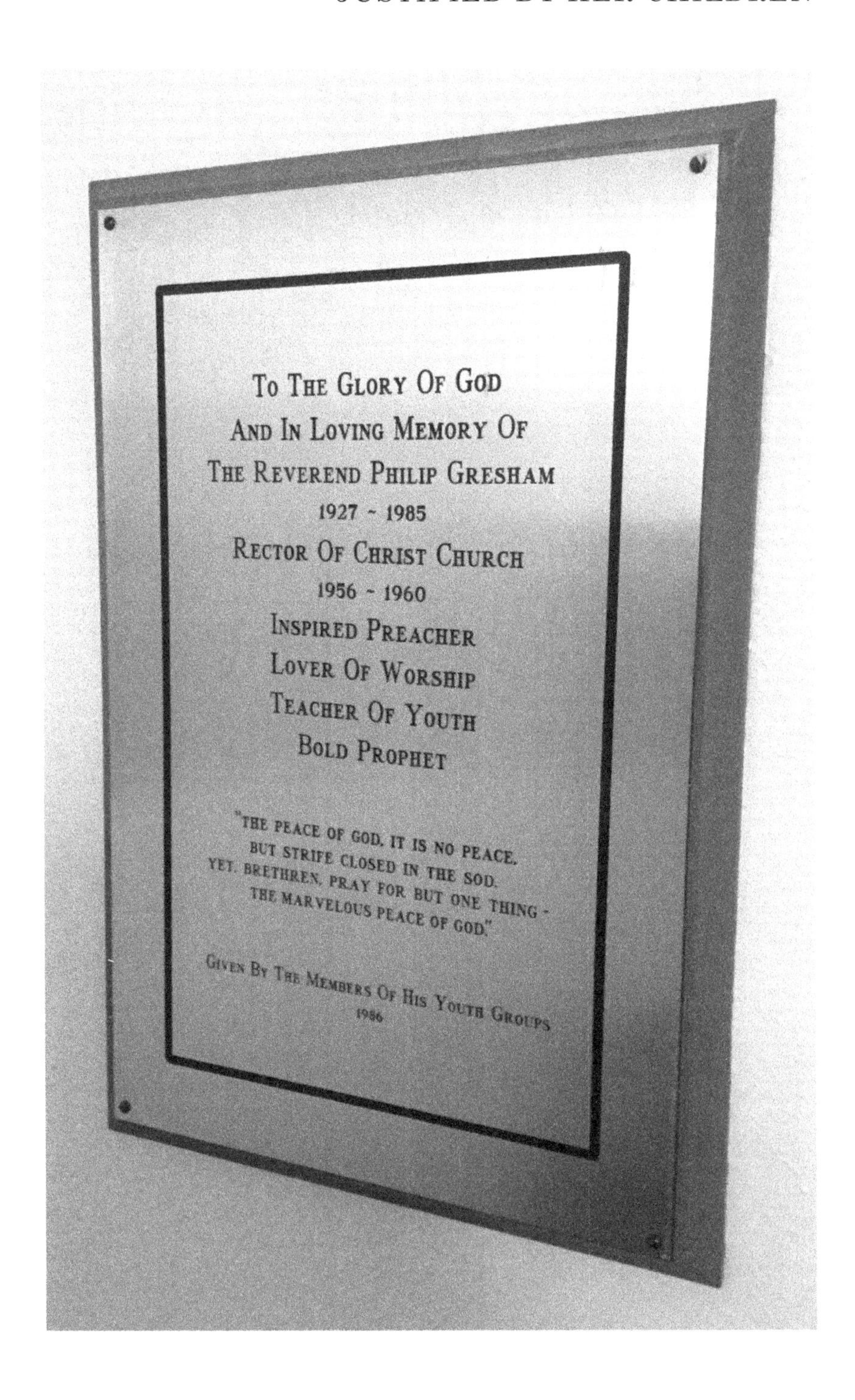
To The Glory Of God
And In Loving Memory Of
The Reverend Philip Gresham
1927 - 1985
Rector Of Christ Church
1956 - 1960
Inspired Preacher
Lover Of Worship
Teacher Of Youth
Bold Prophet
"The peace of God, it is no peace,
but strife closed in the sod.
Yet, brethren, pray for but one thing -
the marvelous peace of God."
Given By The Members Of His Youth Groups
1986

Epilogue

In 2003, The Episcopal Church elected its first openly gay bishop, Gene Robinson of New Hampshire. In 2015, Bishop Michael Curry of North Carolina was elected the first African-American Presiding Bishop of the Episcopal Church.

Discussion Guide

The best discussion questions are the ones that are generated spontaneously from the material. This section exists only as a prompt. The questions are not intended to be the first, only, or the best question for yourself or for your group.

CHAPTER 1

Choir Practice Ambush

1. The author writes about the "cognitive dissonance between what we believe and what we choose to remember." The father at the baptismal instruction remembers his uncle Billy as a good Christian and a member of the KKK. Do you believe it is possible for Uncle Billy to be both? The author introduces us to a community that he will soon discover has issues it does not want him to examine very closely. Can you think of current issues in today's society that cause people to experience "cognitive dissonance"?

2. Titles were often denied minorities as a sign of their inferior status. Phil Gresham asked Charlie to address him by his preferred title, Father, rather than Mister. How do you feel about using titles—Doctor, Judge, Officer, Pastor, etc.—when addressing others? How should children be taught to address their elders? Does a disparity in age between the speaker or the one being addressed make a difference when using a title?

3. What do you know about the role of local and national religious institutions during the Civil Rights struggles of the 1950s and 1960s? Did it matter whether the institution was predominately white or black, Christian or non-Christian, northern or southern?

CHAPTER 2
Virginia is for Lovers

1. Is the honor given men like George Washington and Thomas Jefferson diminished because they were slave owners? What about the honor given to Confederate generals like Robert E. Lee or politicians like Jefferson Davis?

2. The Freedman's Bureau helped the newly freed slaves adjust to life away from the plantation. Is there still a need and/or an obligation to help the descendants of slavery and those who suffered under Jim Crowe laws with reparations?

3. The author relates that as he tried to understand his Southwest Virginia parish, he talked to a number of parishioners now in their 70s who still remembered the young rector from 50-some years ago as "the greatest

priest they ever knew." Do you think of someone whom you remember—or will remember—as the most important influence in your life? What made him or her great?

CHAPTER 3

"People Would Not Understand 'How It Was'"

1. Does your church or family have favorite stories from the past that are valued and repeated as part of its heritage?

2. Biblical scholars will often refer to the *sitz im leben* when discussing a happening, story or parable. This German phrase can be translated as "setting in life," that is, the social context in effect when an episode happens or a story was told. When told that the author intended to write about the gift of the crozier, he was warned that "People would not understand 'How it was.'" Can you think of any examples of a story or happening that you heard or told about where people failed to understand how it was?

3. Studies of social behavior sometimes point out that families and communities can have a code of silence that stifles discussion of difficult subjects. The studies show that the code of silence can arise from feelings of guilt or shame that a family or community doesn't want to own or address. Are there examples of this response in social or community situations today?

CHAPTER 4

Revisiting How It Was

1. The author states, "the racial milieu of the southern states of the old Confederacy was qualitatively different from that of the rest of the country." Do you agree or disagree with the author's statement? Why?

2. Do you accept or reject the proposition that subtle racism exists such as the one describe by the author's story of the ice cream cone? Have you ever experienced subtle racism?

3. Proponents of school vouchers say vouchers allow students, black or white, to escape failing schools while opponents regard school vouchers as a new twist on the tuition grants of massive resistance. Do you believe school vouchers will increase or decrease school integration? Increase or decrease the quality of education for everyone?

4. The new Martinsville High School opened on an integrated basis and chose to forgo the election of a homecoming queen in order to keep racial harmony. Do you believe that was a fair decision for the female students who would look forward to such events?

CHAPTER 5

A New Priest for Christ Episcopal Church

1. How important is a religious understanding to American democracy? How important are a Judaeo-Christian

principles to our understanding of our civic duty as Americans or do other principles apply?

2. The 1st Amendment to the US Constitution states Congress shall make no law respecting an establishment of religion, or prohibiting the free exercise thereof. How strictly should that be amendment be interpreted. Should it allow prayer is schools? At the beginning of government meetings? Pay for military chaplains? Permit the refusal to dispense birth control on religious grounds?

3. Do you see a hierarchy of faith in America today? What religion, denomination, or group has a more favored status? Christianity? Judaism? Islam? Secular non-religious? Evangelical? Mormon? Roman Catholic? Other?

4. Like all nonprofit organizations, churches depend on their membership to choose new leaders. Have you, your church or organization been involved in a call process? What has been your experience of success? How did you find the call process? Easy? Difficult? Overly long? Unnecessarily complicated? In describing your church or organization to candidates was the racial make up its membership part of the description?

CHAPTER 6

Getting Ready for the New rector

1. The New Testament word often translated as priest is presbyter, meaning elder. How important is age and pastoral experience when calling rector or pastor? Is there age discrimination (too young or too old) in the calling process?

Is there a bias in the calling process for men, women, gay, straight, married, single, families with children, tall or short, black, white, or minority? How would you describe the leadership balance in your church when in comes to age, gender, race, etc.

2. What is the optimal tenure of the pastor of a congregation? What are the signs that a minister has stayed too long? Does it injure a congregation when a minister leaves too soon?

3. Denominations differ in line of authority in the church. Some clergy serve at the pleasure of a bishop, some at the pleasure of the church board. Some have renewable contracts while others are essentially tenured positions, and still others are self-employed in a church under their sole control? What checks and balances are best in a church authority? How should authority be shared between the pastor and the congregation on matters of theology, liturgy, personnel, finance, others?

CHAPTER 7

Legacy of Guilt

1. In the early 1960s, Dr. Martin Luther King Jr. called 11 a.m. on Sunday morning, an hour when many Americans are in church, the most segregated hour in the nation. Is that still true today? What if anything has changed?

2. In the nineteenth century Christian denominations split, North and South, over the issue of slavery. The Southern Baptists still exist; the Methodist split lasted almost 100 years. The Episcopal Church did not split over this moral

issue. What weight does unity deserve in deciding moral questions? Recent denominational splits have arisen over the ordination of women and LGBT considerations in marriage & ordination. Do any of these issues outweigh denominational unity?

3. The Rev. Gresham arrived in Martinsville during what is now studied as the Jim Crow era of race relations in this country. What evidence of Jim Crow appears in the social, legal, and cultural structure of the city of Martinsville, the parish of Christ Church, the diocese, and the Commonwealth of Virginia? Is there any residual effect of Jim Crow still operative in society?

CHAPTER 8

Hemlock Haven

1. Bishop Marmion made it clear that diocesan meetings should be racially mixed and should take place in venues where that could occur. He indicated that finding such places was not an easy task. Are there private clubs, associations, organizations, etc., in your area that are not racially mixed? If yes, why is that the case?

2. In talking about integration, Bishop Marmion made the statement, "Sometimes we have difficulty getting our Colored brethren to cooperate after we have gone to great lengths to make it possible for them to experience full fellowship with us." He did not explain what he meant. What do you think he meant?

3. Christ Church was considered a cardinal parish in the diocese. To what degree or in what circumstances should all churches in an organization be treated the same? Treated differently? Should large churches, rich churches, small churches, poor churches, minority churches, mission churches have the same say in the policy of and/or support of the diocese or denominational organization?

CHAPTER 9

"The Best Priest Ever"

1. How much time and energy should the pastor of a congregation give to community events and organizations? Is the time volunteering to serve on boards and attend events considered working for the church? Does a congregation have a say about which organizations its minister can join or support?

2. Churches devote much time and effort to attract young people to church activities. Not all of the adults were pleased when Christ Church added a jukebox and attempted to add a pool table. From rock and roll to rap, the listening habits of young people has been a target of racial attack. To what extent do you think racial prejudice was at play in the parents' objection to a jukebox? Is racial discord still a factor in the criticism of contemporary music popular with young people today?

3. The joke in Texas asks how someone becomes a high school principal. The answer is that a principal was a football coach with a losing season. Sports were an important component of Martinsville High School. Are sports in school given

not enough or too much emphasis as an element of student life? Do you see sports as promoting or narrowing racial understanding?

CHAPTER 10

Bishop William Henry Marmion

1. There were times when enslaving a person was legal and a time when drinking a beer was illegal. Can you name an action that you consider immoral but is not against the law? Can you name a law that you believe is immoral?

2. To replace Judas Iscariot a twelfth Apostle, Matthias was chosen by lot. Roman Catholic bishops were once selected by the king; today the pope alone selects who will be a Catholic bishop. Franklin Graham succeeded his father, Billy, and Joel Olsteen succeeds his father, John, in the leadership of their respective mega-ministries. The Episcopal Church has a search committee name candidates and then a convention of clergy and lay persons elect a bishop. What is the best way to make this important leadership decision?

3. Maya Angelou said, "I think a hero is any person really intent on making this a better place for all people." The subtitle of this book is "Deeds of Courage Confronting a Tradition of Racism." How will you determine if any of the characters are "heroes" or any of their deeds "heroic"?

CHAPTER 11

Cardinal Parish, Cardinal Rector

1. An article in the Episcopal magazine *The Living Church* stated that it was the opinion of many priests and bishops, "that a parish which exceeds 500 communicants has moved across the line, which separates a family from a mob." What is the ideal size of a congregation? Why?

2. Christ Church was faced with the choice of expanding where it was or moving to a different larger location. When should a church expand in place? Move? Start a new congregation?

3. Christendom is the word that is used when, at a time or place, the Christian religion has dominated politics and society. Some Christians long for the return of Christendom while others believe that such accommodation of Christianity to society and the political order eventually perverts the Good News of Christ. How do you see Christianity's role in society and with the political structure?

CHAPTER 12

"Some Mighty Fine Christians..."

1. The author makes a distinction between power and authority. Do you agree with his analysis? Do you agree that leadership includes all but inevitable risk of disappointing those who follow?

2. In his letter to his bishop, Gresham makes the statement, "Some mighty fine Christians are segregationists." How do you react to that statement? Does it matter that it was made

by a priest? Does it matter that it was made in 1958 and not today?

3. The senior warden of Christ Church was a justice on the state supreme court who would have taken an oath to uphold the laws of Virginia. In their letter to the bishop, the vestry states that the integration of Hemlock Haven is "in the violation of the laws of the Commonwealth." How do you see his moral obligations as a Christian, a church senior warden, and a judge?

4. Toward the end of the Vestry resolution it reads: "We feel the above is in keeping with Christian reasoning in that the intermingling of the races, in addition to being illegal, can, in our view, only lead to bitterness, discord, and confusion among our people, which will be a greater 'sin' than that pronounced by judicial decree." What do you make of the argument that they are trying to avoid "bitterness, discord, and confusion"? How do you evaluate the moral position of this resolution?

CHAPTER 13

A Diocese in Turmoil

1. The executive board voiced concern about the impact the integration of Hemlock Haven would have upon the finances of the diocese. Do you feel that conversation about money was appropriate when discussing the propriety of racial integration for the church? Explain your reasons?

2. Throughout the struggle over integration of Hemlock Haven the line between the clergy and the lay leadership was

clearly drawn. Why do you believe this division existed and was so sharp?

3. Do you see any connection between the vote to refuse women a place on church vestries and the vote to refuse to integrate Hemlock Haven?

4. Many of the clergy saw integration as a moral and spiritual matter while many of the laity saw integration as a policy matter. How do you see it?

CHAPTER 14

"The Unfortunate Controversy Which Has Arisen"

1. Phil Gresham apparently believes, "...that a parish not in tension is not, in our day, a Christian parish." Do you agree or disagree that was true in the 1950s? How about today?

2. Gresham's writes in *The Living Church* article, "To claim that the Churchman who is a segregationist is not a Christian is bigotry." How does this fit with your understanding of what it means to be a Christian?

3. The diocesan council voted to shut down the summer youth camp because a majority of the lay delegates did not want racial integration. Should the clergy have refused on moral grounds to participate in segregated youth activities like those at Natural Bridge where only young white people were permitted?

4. It would be fair to characterize the senior warden's resolution to the vestry as his hope that the unfortunate controversy of integration be removed from church consideration and that the church move forward with Christ's work. Can you name political-social questions that should be disconnected from religion? Do you think a church can avoid divisive social and/or moral issues and be faithful to the gospel?

CHAPTER 15
Movers and Shakers

1. Francis West was a leading member of the opposition to Bishop Marmion. His letter shows the political maneuvering that went on before and at diocesan council. Do you believe this type of politicking is normal or exceptional in church governance? Does it have a place in how things get done in a church?

2. Many countries have abolished the death penalty. Should a sentence of death have a place in our judicial system? What about for crimes that do not involve the death of another?

3. It was argued that, even if the men were guilty, the execution of seven persons for a crime that did not include the death of the victim was not fair or serve justice. Do you agree? Do you believe the race of the victim and/or the defendant influenced the sentence?

CHAPTER 16

A Gift for the Bishop

1. At the winter youth conference, a straw vote was taken, and by a three to one majority, the young people attending said "they would attend youth conferences on a non-segregated basis." Why do you think their reaction was so different from the adult church delegates at Council?

2. The Fifth Commandment of the Ten Commandments requires us to honor our parents, yet the Christ Church youth group was taking a stand for racial equality in direct opposition to the leaders of their church. Should they be admired or criticized for this action? Did Charlie Cole make the correct moral decision to obey his father and not read the Manifesto at the 1959 annual congregational meeting?

3. Bishop Heath Light's comment asks us to ponder an important question, "How is it possible to reconcile how the vehement racist attitudes existed in a church that regularly invited the era's greatest Christian theologians to speak at its Laymen's League?"

CHAPTER 17

Race is the Issue

1. The Rev. Jack Teeter resigned because he believed the vestry "would refuse to let a fellow Christian vote as his prayers and conscience direct him to." Do you believe it is the responsibility of elected representatives to vote the popular opinion of their constituents or to follow their conscience? Is it different for unelected leaders such as pastors of a church?

2. Doctrine can be defined as belief based on higher authority such as scripture or ancient church tradition while policy can be defined as adopted principles of action. Was racial integration a matter of doctrine or policy?

3. One lay delegate stated, "The clergy has failed to sell the laymen on integration." Was it the job of the clergy to "sell" the laity on integration or, as some contended, was it wrong for them to even try?

CHAPTER 18

Maybe the Issue Wasn't Just Race

1. In the 50 years from 1967, the year the Supreme Court ruled in Loving v. Virginia that interracial marriage was constitutional, and by 2017 marriage between partners of different races grew from 3 percent to 17 percent. Is there a stigma attached to interracial marriage today? What changes occurred to make interracial marriage more common? Are there still challenges for interracial couples?

2. During the Gulf War, a priest was asked by a parishioner if he was for the war. The priest replied, "Do you want your priest to be for war?" The Rev. Frank Vest's parishioner was against integration but did not want his priest to agree with that position. In the 1950s, a priest getting a divorce was required to offer his resignation to the vestry. How common is it for people to have one moral standard for civil life and another moral standard for church life? Should there be different expectations?

3. The black delegates to diocesan council who vigorously worked for the racial integration of Hemlock Haven felt insulted by the proposals that the racial integration of their children might come only at the price of segregation by gender. Do you think the proposal was reasonable compromise or an unreasonable insult?

CHAPTER 19

"An Unhappy Business That God Has Given"

1. The lay leadership of Christ Church made its opposition to integration very clear. Gresham was not in agreement with their position. Some members of the congregation showed their resistance to this position by a contribution to the Builders for Christ fund. What opinion about the racial sentiments of the Christ Church membership have you formed so far? Does a church's membership tend to reflect the attitude of their lay leaders or their pastor?

2. Opposition to Gresham's leadership began to develop on several fronts. There was grumbling about his liturgical style, his permissive attitude toward the youth group, and his irreverence with regard to church customs. Do you think that these issues would have been overlooked if Gresham had backed his leadership on racial segregation?

3. Is it too easy or too difficult to dissolve the relationship between a church's pastor and the congregation? Does a bishop tend to favor the priest, the congregation, or remain neutral?

CHAPTER 20

The Crozier Arrives

1. How important are church appointments and adornments to your worship? Do national flags belong in a church? What about banners? Such as: Black Lives Matter banner? Choose Life banner? Gay Pride banner?

2. To what extent should a church attempt to beautify a church building or worship services when there are so many poor, homeless, and hungry people? What do you think when you see a grand church in a poor neighborhood?

3. A crozier is the traditional symbol of the office of bishop. How important are symbols to you? Wedding rings? Standing for the national anthem? Statues in a park?

CHAPTER 21

A Refutation of God's Teachings

1. A father of the congregation wrote the vestry objecting to an invitation his children received to a box supper that would include both black and white children. Is it noteworthy that his children were two daughters rather than sons and he referred to the box supper as a Negro-White Social? He referred to Gresham's notification as a deception although the diocesan policy for five years was to have integrated meetings where possible. Why do you think this policy never registered with some in the diocese?

2. Did the vestry overreact in its reaction to the letter about the integrated box supper? What other steps could it have taken in response to the letter?

3. Was resignation Gresham's best response to the vestry's actions? What is your opinion on Gresham's comment to the vestry that with their views on race, it would be unlikely that any priest "of the caliber necessary to the continuation and carrying on of the present work of the parish" would accept their call to become rector?

CHAPTER 22
Down by the Hemlock

1. The vestry writes to the congregation that "Unless we keep the lines of communication open to one another, understanding and unity will be impossible" and at the same time writes, "We feel that debate on these recent events will accomplish nothing but rather may lead to further division, consequently we urge each of you to try and forget that which is past—except to profit by our experiences—and to proceed with singleness of Christian purpose with the work at hand." How do you believe was the overall goal in writing this letter? What is your overall opinion of this letter?

2. The vestry claimed to not know why Gresham resigned despite the minutes of the vestry's May 4th meeting and their letter to the congregation both reference Gresham's belief that the vestry's actions were a refutation of God's teachings and the policy of the church. Do you think they did not accept his belief as sufficient reason for resignation? The vestry was willing to view the disagreements with

Gresham over racial integration as a difference of opinion. Should Gresham have viewed it this way?

3. The vestry letter states that it deplored the involvement of the diocese in a sociological problem that was also politically explosive. What are the sociological/political problems that the church is involved with today? That it has mostly avoided today?

CHAPTER 23

The Peace Offering

1. It is not known whether any African-American children attended the integrated box supper that led to Gresham's resignation. Does that matter in forming your opinion about the actions taken by Gresham and the vestry?

2. Why do you believe the all-male diocesan council was unable to adopt a resolution opening Hemlock Haven to all baptized members of Hemlock Haven when the Episcopal Church Women and the Episcopal Young Churchmen passed resolutions urging them to do so?

3. Multiple resolutions for gradual integration were proposed and defeated at the 1960 diocesan council. Is complete rejection of an immoral situation the only acceptable solution or is it permissible to accept a partial solution to a moral issue? Can you give an example for your answer?

CHAPTER 24

"My Heart is Still There"

1. Were you surprised to read that rather than react with anger at Christ Church, Gresham missed "that wonderful parish in Martinsville, and those dear, grand people?" Is it possible to agree with Gresham's assessment of the parish and its people? To disagree?

2. With what you have read about the brief rectorship of Philip Gresham at Christ Church do you believe he was the right man for that church? Why? What should he have done differently?

3. In his article in *The Living Church*, Gresham encouraged priests to stay in their parishes despite the tensions over racial integration. Do you believe Gresham did the right thing in resigning from Christ Church?

4. Do you believe Gresham could have had a successful ministry if he had stayed at Christ Church? If there were irreconcilable differences at Christ Church between the leadership and Gresham, is the blame for their falling out equally shared or is one party more accountable for the breakup?

CHAPTER 25

"The Arc of the Moral Universe is Long..."

1. Jere Bunting was described as to the vestry as a priest who would not challenge them on racial issues. Jack Teeter was

caught on film being forcibly ejected from the courtroom when he attempted to sit in the section reserved for Negro spectators. Is either priest a better example of Christian witness to the world? Which priest would you rather have as rector of your church? Why?

2. Was Bishop Marmion's decision to retract Jack Teeter's appointment to St. Paul's Church necessary to keep peace in the diocese and with Christ Church or a mistake for giving in to unreasonable demands?

3. The author states, "In different places in different eras, the established authority of an oppressor was challenged by the moral force of marginalized instigators." How do you view instigators? Necessary for change? Problematic for those working for change? Are there good instigators and bad instigators? Give examples of good and/or bad instigators?

CHAPTER 26

"...But it Bends Towards Justice"

1. The author writes," People cannot be blamed for what they cannot know." To what degree can the characters of this book be held accountable or excused for their actions based on their knowledge of the sin of racism?

2. The author gives an example of a congregation who believes their preacher went from preaching to meddling. To what degree do you expect your church to guide you in your moral behavior? In sociological problems? Marriage? Club membership? Sexual relationships? Investments?

3. How well do you think the church has confronted its tradition of racism? What more needs to be done?

Endnotes

Common abbreviations in these Endnotes: *MVL Bulletin* is the *Martinsville Bulletin* newspaper; VM refers to the vestry Minutes of Christ Episcopal Church; MAVAHI is the Yearbook for Martinsville High School, CEC refers to Christ Episcopal Church in Martinsville, VA; *RT* refers to the *Roanoke Times* newspaper; *RW* refers to the *Roanoke World News* newspaper.

Chapter 1

1. ff interview, Charlie Cole
2. Donald Trump statement to media August 15, 2017, about Charlottesville protest
3. *The Washington Post,* July 18, 2019, "The psychological phenomenon that blinds Trump supporters to his racism," Kathleen D. Vohs

Chapter 2

4. *The Hairstons,* Henry Wienck, p. 49
5. *The Hairstons,* p. 8
6. *The Hairstons,* p. 193–194
7. *Prominent families of Patrick & Henry County,* p. 84–86
8. Archival newspaper article 1956 announcing arrival of Gresham and interview with Sue Rosser

9. Unsigned biography of Philip Gresham from CEC Archives, probably written by Ed Covert

Chapter 4

10. *MVL Bulletin,* Jan. 13, 2016
11. Martinsville Chamber of Commerce website & Lexington, NC, newspaper *The Dispatch,* June 29, 1998
12. Martinsville's Chamber of Commerce website
13. *The Dispatch* (Lexington, NC), June 27, 1998
14. Wikipedia mentions the nukes but that is an often-told story in Martinsville
15. Encyclopedia of VA (internet), Massive Resistance, https://www.encyclopediavirginia.org/massive_resistance
16. Television News of the Civil Rights Era 1950–1970 Website Copyright William G. Thomas, III and rector and Board of Visitors, University of Virginia. All Rights Reserved. 2005. http://www2.vcdh.virginia.edu/civilrightstv/
17. Virginia Historical Society website: Massive Resistance. https://www.virginiahistory.org/collections-and-resources/virginia-history-explorer/civil-rights-movement-virginia/massive
18. Ibid.
19. Ibid.
20. Ibid.
21. Ibid.
22. http://albertharrishighalumni.org
23. MAVAHI 1970 school blog

Chapter 5

24. Franklin D. Roosevelt's Address to Congress, January 6, 1941
25. *American Gospel: God, the Founding Fathers, and the Making of a Nation,* Jon Meacham, p. 177
26. Website of TEC and Diocese of VA
27. *Hills of the Lord,* Katherine L. Brown
28. William Temple visited Christ Church Martinsville when he was Archbishop of York (1942–1945)
29. History of CEC on their website
30. Men of Christ Church history, CEC archives

31. Ibid.
32. Uncredited CEC Archive photocopy of news article
33. VM, 6/3/1956. Present at this meeting were "Senior Warden Kennon C Whittle and Junior Warden F. V. Woodson, vestrymen M. B. Hesdorffer, Warren J. Watrous, Escole W. Burroughs, M. K. Jacobs, Edwin G. Penn, R. M. Simmons Sr., R. M. Simmons Jr., Clarence H. Burrage, Robert B. Mercer, Dr. Paul Turner Jr., H. Kenneth Whitener, Clarence P. Kearfott, B. S. Parrish, and W. H. Yeaman."
34. Letter in CEC Archive
35. VM, 7/5/1956
36. VM, 8/13/1956
37. VM, 7/5/1956
38. VM, 8/13/56
39. Marmion letter 5/27/1960 We do not know exactly Gresham's compensation when hired other than it equaled Fishburne's. We know approximately what Gresham was making when he left CEC.

Chapter 6

40. Philip Gresham's obituary called him a Richmond, VA, native.
41. VMI had a pre-induction program for the army. This may be what is referenced here.
42. Access to Archival Database (AAD)
43. Unsigned undated letter from CEC Archives
44. Unsigned biography of Philip Gresham from CEC Archives probably written by Ed Covert
45. Clipping of newspaper account of Gresham's arrival at CEC 1956, CEC Archive
46. CEC archives, uncredited newspaper clip, "New Episcopal Church Rector Takes up Duties Tomorrow"
47. VM, 8/13/1956
48. VM, 8/13/1956
49. CEC bulletin, 9/9/1956
50. VM, 9/16/1956
51. VM, 9/23/1956
52. Interview with Ann Gardner
53. CEC Bulletin, 10/14/1956

54. News clipping, 10/21/1956, CEC Archives
55. Martin Luther King Jr., "Social Justice and the Emerging New Age" address, Western Michigan University, 1963

Chapter 7

56. http://christchurchmvl.org/info/Celebrate.cfm
57. http://www.episcopalarchives.org/Afro-Anglican_history/exhibit/transitions/inclusive_episcopate.php
58. http://www.episcopalarchives.org/Afro-Anglican_history/exhibit/divergence/ccwacp.php
59. http://www.episcopalarchives.org/Afro-Anglican_history/exhibit/escru/index.php
60. unsigned History of St. Paul's, CEC archives
61. The *Roanoke Times* refers to five such churches; Christ Church's vestry minutes mentions only 4. VM, 10/27/1956
62. http://www.episcopalarchives.org/Afro-Anglican_history/exhibit/escru/sewanee.php
63. http://www.sewanee.edu/about/university-history/
64. http://www.sewanee.edu/about/university-history/

Chapter 8

65. *Journal of the Diocese of SWVA,* 1955
66. VM, 10/27/1956
67. VM, 4/2/1957
68. VM, 6/5/1957
69. VM, 7/3/1957
70. VM, 8/7/1957
71. VM, 9/4/1957

Chapter 9

72. Martinsville-Henry County Chamber of Commerce website
73. The Lester Family Facebook
74. CEC Bulletin, 10/14/1956
75. News clipping, 11/5/56, CEC Archives
76. VM, 12/4/1957
77. News clipping, undated, CEC Archives
78. Swezey Interview
79. Ann Gardner Interview

80. Swezey Interview
81. VM, 12/4/1957
82. Ann Gardner Interview
83. Swezey Interview
84. MAVAHI yearbook, 1958
85. MAVAHI yearbook, 1960
86. Swezey Interview
87. Charlie Cole Interview

Chapter 10

88. *The Living Church,* Vol. 136, No. 26, June 29, 1958, "Unhealed Wound," Philip Gresham
89. *Southwestern Episcopalian,* 12/1953
90. "Race & The Episcopal Church: A Dance along the Path to Racial Equality" presented by Nina Salmon at Phoebe Needles, 9/13/2014
91. *Southwestern Episcopalian,* 12/1953
92. *Southwestern Episcopalian,* 12/1953
93. St. Mark's Episcopal Church Website
94. *Hills of the Lord,* p. 126
95. *Southwestern Episcopalian,* 12/1953
96. *Southwestern Episcopalian,* 6/1954
97. Archival clipping with note "The *Roanoke Times.*" Attending the ceremony from Martinsville were the Senior Warden, Justice Kennon Whittle and his wife, Bishop Calling committee member, Fred V. Woodson and his wife, Superintendent of the Sunday school Beverly S. Parrish Sr., Rives Brown Sr., President of the Laymen's League, Charles C. Broun, President of the Women's Auxiliary, Mrs. William R. Windle, President of the Youth League, Miss Georgiana Jacobs, alternative to the Electing Council, Clarence Kearfott, chairman of the Altar Guild, Miss Flora Whittle, Past President of the Women's Auxiliary, Mrs. Henkel Price and member of the Diocesan Department of Christian Education Mrs. Ruth Swiger.
98. *RT,* 5/14/1954, CEC archives

Chapter 11

99. VM, 6/5/1957
100. VM, 6/23/1957
101. Atkinson letter of 7/9/1957
102. VM, 5/17/1958
103. VM, 12/10/1958
104. *MVL Bulletin,* Stroller article credit to Virginia Waddle
105. National Register of Historic Places, VDHR file no. 120–6
106. National Register of Historic Places VDHR file no. 120–6
107. VM, 5/13/1959
108. VM, 5/13/1959

Chapter 12

109. Thanks to Hugh O'Doherty, of the John F Kennedy School of Government, for this insight
110. VM, 3/4/1957
111. Gresham letter to Marmion, 3/4/1958. Bill Reardon referred to in the letter is the Venerable B. Clifton Reardon, Archdeacon of the diocese.
112. VM, 3/8/1958. Hemlock Haven is near the village of Smyth, VA
113. *RT,* 3/23/1958
114. Newspaper clipping, CEC Archives
115. Newspaper clipping, CEC Archives
116. Newspaper clipping, CEC Archives
117. Newspaper clipping, CEC Archives
118. *Florence Times,* 3/24/1958
119. *MVL Bulletin,* 5/6/1960

Chapter 13

120. Minutes of the Executive Board of SWVA, 4/17/1958. All quotes for this meeting are from the minutes.
121. *RT,* 5/18/1958
122. *Southwestern Episcopalian,* Sept. 1969, p. 18
123. *RW,* 5/16/1958
124. *RT,* 5/17/1958
125. *RW,* 5/16/1958
126. *RW,* 5/16/1958

127. Journal of the 39th Annual Council
128. *RW,* 5/16/1958
129. *Southwestern Episcopalian,* June 1958
130. *RW,* 5/16/1958
131. *Southwestern Episcopalian,* June 1958
132. *RW,* 5/16/1958
133. Journal of the 39th Annual Council
134. *Southwestern Episcopalian,* June 1958
135. *RT,* 5/18/1958
136. *Southwestern Episcopalian,* June 1958
137. *Southwestern Episcopalian,* June 1958. Does make one wonder about the absence of laymen for this vote.
138. VM, 5/1/1957
139. *RT,* 5/17/1958
140. *RT,* 5/18/1958. Quotes of Locher & Whitehead

Chapter 14

141. VM, 06/04/1958
142. Comment by Lucy Davis
143. MAVAHI Yearbook, 1958, 1959, & 1960
144. MAVAHI Yearbook, 1959 & 1960
145. Sunday Bulletin, CEC Recognition Sunday 2013
146. Virginia Tech website
147. "The Spirit of the Award," CEC archives
148. Sue Rosser Interview
149. *The Living Church,* Vol.136, No. 26, June 29, 1958, "Unhealed Wound," Philip Gresham
150. All quotations in this paragraph and the next are taken from *The Living Church,* Vol. 136, No. 26, June 29, 1958, "Unhealed Wound," Philip Gresham
151. "Race & The Episcopal Church: A Dance along the Path to Racial Equality" presented by Nina Salmon at Phoebe Needles, 9/13/2014
152. VM, 10/24/1958
153. VM, 12/10/1958

Chapter 15

154. John Swezey interview

155. Diocesan Archive letter from West. The Evans House referred to in the letter is the diocesan headquarters housing the bishop's office
156. *History of Patrick and Henry Counties, Virginia,* Virginia G. & Lewis G. Pedigo
157. *MVL Bulletin,* 11/10/1967
158. *MVL Bulletin,* 2/18/1949
159. *The Martinsville Seven and Southern Justice: Race, Crime, and Capital Punishment in Virginia, 1949–1951,* Eric Walter Rise
160. Ibid. The Martinsville Seven
161. *MVL Bulletin,* 4/19/1949
162. *MVL Bulletin,* 4/20/1949
163. *Richmond Times Dispatch,* 2/6/2011
164. *MVL Bulletin,* 4/22/1949
165. *Communist Daily Worker,* 6/12/1949
166. *MVL Bulletin,* 4/19/1949
167. *MVL Bulletin,* 4/19/1949
168. Ibid. The Martinsville Seven
169. *MVL Bulletin,* 9/6/1949
170. Ibid. The Martinsville Seven
171. Ibid. The Martinsville Seven
172. *MVL Bulletin,* opinion reprint 5/16/1949
173. *New Leader,* "The Martinsville Rape Case," Henry Lee Moon, 2/12/1951
174. *Richmond African-American,* 8/5/50
175. *New Leader,* "The Martinsville Rape Case" by Henry Lee Moon 2/12/1951
176. *Richmond African-American,* 7/15/1950
177. *Richmond Times Dispatch,* 2/6/2011

Chapter 16

178. Calculated using a lunar calendar, the Jewish calendar of Jesus' time, Easter is a movable feast occurring as early as March 22 and as late as April 25. The Feast of the Resurrection of Jesus, Easter's proper name, is always the first Sunday after the full moon that occurs after the equinox.

179. Carnival is derived from two Latin words often translated, "Farewell to meat (flesh)."
180. Interviews with John Swezey & Sue Rosser
181. Letter to the Smyrnaeans
182. Book of Common Prayer 1928, p. 543
183. *Encyclopedia of Religion in the South,* Samuel S. Hill, Charles H. Lippy, Charles Reagan Wilson, p. 832
184. Unsigned letter from CEC Archives
185. John Swezey & Ann Gardner Interviews
186. John Swezey Interview
187. *The Living Church,* Vol. 136, No. 26, June 29, 1958, "Unhealed Wound," Philip Gresham
188. *RT,* May 12, 1960, article by Melville Carico
189. John Swezey Interview
190. Matthew 13:14

Chapter 17

191. 2/26/1959 AP Article from Newspaper clip, CEC Archive
192. 2/26/1959 AP Article from Newspaper clip, CEC Archive
193. 2/26/1959 AP Article from Newspaper clip, CEC Archive
194. *Jet Magazine,* 4/30/1959
195. *Jet Magazine,* 4/30/1959
196. "Paved with Good Intentions: The Road to Racial Unity in the Episcopal Diocese of Southwestern Virginia" by Nina Salmon
197. *RT,* 4/17/1959
198. *RT,* 4/17/1959
199. *RT,* 4/17/1959
200. *RT,* 4/17/1959
201. *Southwestern Episcopalian,* May 1959
202. *RT,* 4/17/1959
203. *RT,* 4/17/1959
204. *Southwestern Episcopalian,* May 1959 (although the *Roanoke Times* 4/17/59 reported the resolution was tabled)
205. *RT,* 4/17/1959
206. *RT,* 4/17/1959
207. *Southwestern Episcopalian,* May 1959
208. *Southwestern Episcopalian,* May 1959
209. *RT,* 4/17/1959

Chapter 18

210. VM, 5/13/1959
211. US Supreme Court, *Loving v. Virginia,* 388 US 1
212. *Episcopalians and Race: Civil War to Civil Rights,* Gardiner H. Shattuck Jr., p. 106
213. "Race & The Episcopal Church: A Dance along the Path to Racial Equality" presented by Nina Salmon at Phoebe Needles, 9/13/2014
214. *RT,* 1/15/1961
215. Undated newspaper clip from *Roanoke Times* but probably May 1960, CEC Archives
216. Bishop Heath Light Interview
217. *RT,* 5/18/1960
218. "Race & The Episcopal Church: A Dance along the Path to Racial Equality" presented by Nina Salmon at Phoebe Needles, 9/13/2014
219. Trippi Penn Interview
220. Ann Gardner Interview
221. John Swezey and Charlie Cole Interviews

Chapter 19

222. VM, 5/13/1959
223. VM, 5/13/1959
224. Unsigned letter from Sunday school teacher, CEC Archives
225. Letter to Congregation, 8/25/1958
226. VM, 2/4/1959
227. *MVL Bulletin,* 5/6/1960
228. Ann Gardner and others
229. Sue Rosser Interview
230. Ann Gardner Interview
231. VM, 2/3/1960
232. Interviews with members of CEC
233. Book of Common Prayer 1928, pp. 84–85

Chapter 20

234. Sue Rosser Interview
235. www.silvermakersmarks.co.uk/

Chapter 21

236. CEC Archives, undated unattributed newspaper clip
237. VM, 2/3/1960
238. VM, 4/6/1960
239. VM, 5/4/1960
240. Postcard from CEC archives
241. VM, 5/4/1960

Chapter 22

242. Letter from CEC Archives
243. *MVL Bulletin,* 5/6/1960
244. Gresham to Marmion letter, 5/11/1960
245. VM, 5/11/1960
246. VM, 5/11/1960 & copy of letter, CEC Archives
247. Ann Gardner Interview
248. John Swezey Interview
249. *Milwaukee Sentinel,* 7/2/1960

Chapter 23

250. The *Roanoke Times* uses the number 125 both on 5/17/1958 & 9/28/1962. It may be that this statistic was not well documented by church, well-researched by the newspaper, or both. Communicants would be baptized members over the age of thirteen, younger children would not be included in this number.
251. *Southwestern Episcopalian,* June 1960
252. *RT,* 5/14/1960
253. *Southwestern Episcopalian,* June 1960

Chapter 24

254. Marmion letter to Stokes, 5/16/1960
255. Gresham letter to Marmion, 6/1/1960
256. Marmion letter to Griffiths, 10/4/1960
257. Marmion letter to Griffiths, 10/4/1960
258. Gresham letter to Marmion, 3/3/1961
259. Gresham letter to Marmion, undated but probably 11/1960
260. Marmion letter to Gresham, 11/21/1960
261. Gresham letter to Marmion, 3/3/1961

262. Marmion letter to Gresham, 12/6/1961
263. Gresham letter to Marmion, 1/25/1962
264. Comments of CEC members
265. Clipped obituary, 2/13/1985, believed to be a Richmond newspaper

Chapter 25

266. VM, 6/1/1960
267. Undated Report of the Calling Committee recommending The Rev. Jere Bunting signed by C. P. Kearfott, Chairman
268. VM, 10/5/1960
269. VM, 11/14/1962
270. *RT,* 12/15/1960
271. *News & Advance,* posted online 6/18/2009, "Civil Rights in Central Virginia"
272. Undated film & transcript from WSLS archives
273. *RT,* 2/22/1961
274. VM, 12/13/1962
275. VM, 12/16/1962
276. VM, 12/16/1962
277. VM, 12/19/62
278. VM, 12/23/1962
279. VM, 1/9/1963
280. CEC Archives, undated article *Roanoke Times,* probably May 1962
281. *Times,* 9/28/1962
282. *MVL Bulletin,* 11/10/1967
283. *Magnet,* Ralph C. Lester
284. Undated Report of the Calling Committee recommending The Rev. Jere Bunting signed by C. P. Kearfott, Chairman
285. Robert Jeffress, pastor of First Baptist Church in Dallas, chastised Trump critics who have called his policy of separating families inhumane and unnecessary. "It's absolutely wrong for the president to be called evil for simply fulfilling his God-given responsibility," *Houston Chronicle* article by Monica Rhor, June 22, 2018

Chapter 25

286. Articles of Religion, Article XXI BCP, p. 872
287. Philippians 2:12
288. John Fea, Professor and chair of Early American History, Messiah College. Mars Hill Audio Journal
289. John 8:23
290. Interview with Bishop A. Heath Light
291. Diocesan Annual Report, 1993
292. *Southwestern Episcopalian,* March 1993
293. *RT,* 6/1/2002
294. *Virginia Pilot,* 11/26/2007

About the Author

The Reverend Roy G. Pollina will tell you that he is one of those blessed people who got to be what he wanted to be when he grew up. Since the time he was chosen to lead the prayers at his kindergarten graduation through the years as a choir boy and an acolyte, Roy dreamed of becoming a priest. After receiving his BA at Northern Illinois University in 1973 and his M. Div from the Episcopal Seminary of the Southwest in 1985, Roy was ordained a deacon in that same year and a priest in 1986 by the bishop of Louisiana. After 30 years of leading congregations, Roy retired from Christ Church in Martinsville, Virginia. Roy's first book, *To Bless a Child,* was published by Morehouse Publishing, in 2009. *Justified by her Children* is his second nonfiction book and his first history. Roy and his wife, Susan, enjoy their 6.5 heavily-wooded acres in the mountains of northern Georgia. He continues to do Sunday services for local parishes.

CPSIA information can be obtained
at www.ICGtesting.com
Printed in the USA
JSHW030802260922
30847JS00001B/4